THE
POWER
of
PROPHETIC
TEAMS

by DIANE HARRISON

How to start a prophetic team in your church

THE POWER OF PROPHETIC TEAMS

Copyright © 2017, Diane Harrison

ISBN: 978-1975912451

To order additional copies or

For more information, please contact:

www.dianeharrison.ca

ACKNOWLEDGEMENTS

Cover design by Brian Danchuk, Curve Design—Thank you for the hours invested into this vision.

Copy Editor—Darla Jean Redekopp—Thank you for the hours of sacrifice and support given.

Thank you to my family and the many friends who believed in me all along the way, giving opinions and feedback to keep this project moving forward. Without their constant faith in me I would have faltered and quit.

Thank you to the Harvest City leadership team who have been constant in their encouragement over the years.

Thank you to my husband who has been my coach and cheerleader from the beginning.

REFERENCES

"Diane Harrison is well-qualified to write this book on establishing prophetic teams in local churches. She is an excellent prophetess and leader who over the years has helped many local churches raise up prophetic people and teams. I highly recommend this book which brings much needed clarity and practical instruction to leaders and churches wanting to establish dynamic, healthy, prophetic ministry in their church."

Dave Wells
Team Leader, Life Links International Fellowship,
Regina, SK, Canada

"It has been my pleasure to have been mentored personally in the prophetic ministry from Diane, and to support her in the development of prophetic teams at Harvest City Church. Diane has a tremendous understanding of how prophetic ministry should function within a local church setting, and she writes this book from practical experience and not just a theoretical point of view. Because of Diane's passion for the prophetic and her diligence to train and equip others in this ministry, we have enjoyed a fountain of prophetic blessing at our church for many years. Although Diane is a strong prophetic voice herself, her main desire is to see many other prophetic voices raised up, and to see the prophetic flourish at the local church level. I'm thrilled that Diane has taken the time to put into book format what she has learned and developed over the years in our church, so that many others can learn and be blessed, as we have been."

Joel Wells, Lead Pastor
Harvest City Church
Regina, Sk. Canada

"Diane Harrison's practical knowledge and experience in prophetic ministry is a gift to the Body of Christ. Well spoken and articulate, Diane captures the essence of how to successfully develop prophetic teams and establish a ministry impacting the local church and beyond."

Ian Byrd, Pastor
Church of the Rock
Calgary, Alberta, Canada

"Diane Harrison is a seasoned, trusted, impactful prophetic minister who is also a creative, fruitful and Life-giving coach and equipper of various prophetic ministers and teams. The kind of ministry experience, practical wisdom and sound biblical foundations that she brings to bear on developing effective prophetic ministries are invaluable resources. Her book is a must read for anyone wanting to start a prophetic team or increase the effectiveness of the prophetic in their local church."

Ben Goodman (Prophet)
Manna Church
Fayetteville, North Carolina, USA

"Diane Harrison has a proven and effective prophetic ministry that reaches far beyond her home church. She has coupled her keen ability to hear from God with strong leadership skills to reproduce prophetic ministry in others and build a dynamic prophetic team in her local church. Diane reflects Christ's love for His church. Her warmth and maturity create receptivity and readiness to obey the word of the Lord."

Steve Chupp, Pastor
Harvest Community Church
Goshen, Indiana, USA

"I first heard Diane speak on this subject several years ago and her teaching formed the basis for our own Prophetic Teams in CFC, Belfast.

Her book on the subject is full of biblical truth, intensely practical and well thought out. It isn't weird or wacky but manages to combine flowing in The Spirit with down to earth church protocols. Every pastor will love it!

We couldn't recommend a book more highly. If you want to get the most out of prophetic people and bless the Church, buy a couple of books and spread the word."

Paul Reid, Pastor Emeritus
Christian Fellowship Church
10 Belmont Road, Belfast, Ireland

"Diane Harrison is a mature prophetic gift to the Church, and having known her for well over 20 years, I appreciate her powerful and accurate release of prophecy both to individuals and to local churches.

One of Diane's passions is to see other people raised up and released in prophetic ministry and she has been successful in pioneering and establishing prophetic teams in her local church at Harvest City, Regina.

The Power of Prophetic Teams is a very practical and relevant handbook for anyone who has a desire to see the development of this ministry in their local church.

I highly recommend this valuable tool for anyone who wants to see a greater release of the prophetic ministry."

Phil Cana, Pastor
Sheffield Christian Life Centre
Sheffield, Yorkshire, UK

"For you can all prophesy..." declares the Apostle Paul, writing to Christians in the local church at Corinth. This is the heart-cry of Diane Harrison. She has spent years cultivating prophetic gifting in her own life and in many others, world-wide. In this excellent and practical manual, she shares proven methods, with Biblical guidelines, to equip the saints for a greater distribution of Christ into His church, through timely prophetic words. This book doesn't belong on a shelf!"

Dr. Clem Ferris
International Prophetic Ministry;
Chapel Hill, North Carolina, USA

"This book has been a long time coming! Unlike many Christian books, this is not theory or a "good idea" since Di has been actively working her teachings in her growing local church for more than 20 years.

It has been my privilege to work with her in conferences and in local church prophetic gatherings for many years. We have enjoyed teaching and prophesying together at home and abroad, and her insights into the prophetic in the context of the local church, have made her an invaluable asset and resource, for many leaders seeking to give the Prophetic its rightful place. It has been my privilege to go from coach to co-worker as she has progressed in her Gift.

The book will answer many questions and allow her to leave a legacy of teaching for those that follow. Prophecy and local church do go together and this book will give you the "how to's" for your church."

Keith Hazell, Prophet
Ground Level Associates
Lethbridge, Alberta, Canada

TABLE OF CONTENTS

INTRODUCTION

My husband Todd and I came to faith in Christ in the late seventies, just as the "Jesus people" movement was coming to an end. Todd and I then encountered the power of the Holy Spirit almost as soon as we gave our lives to the Lord. Immediately I was aware of His power within me, but I also encountered the Holy Spirit in another way: I remember praying in our living room—Todd, my mother in law, and I—on the floor (we only had pillows for furniture), and the room being filled with a tremendous white light and the presence of God so thick I could hardly breathe. Today I compare it to a "Book of Acts" experience…Todd and his mom couldn't see the white light the same as I could, so I kept describing it to them. After that encounter, when I would be praying or in a church service, I began to get words coming to me seemingly out of nowhere. Along with the words, I'd have a compulsion to speak them out; I had not heard or seen prophecy, so I just thought this was part of the experience of being a Christian. Shortly after that, I began to see pictures over people when we would pray for them and it was uncomfortable, because of my lack of understanding. I wondered secretly if I was crazy. Fortunately my boss, who had become a friend and mentor, explained that I had a prophetic gift, and that it was written about in the Bible. Before long, I was able to see and hear prophecy being given by others in the charismatic church we were attending, so it didn't seem quite so weird.

Today, more than 30 years later, we have entire teams of prophetically gifted people, organized and working together for God's purposes. As prophetic coordinator at Harvest City Church in Regina,

Saskatchewan, I have never been so enthusiastic about the vibrant growth and development in the lives of those we are mentoring. What a joy to see them become effective prophetic ministers, as we work together in teams, and tune our spirits to hear what God has to say to the person in our chair. God always has a personal love letter that he wants to deposit in each person's heart and spirit. Always. Ministering to people in this way has revolutionized the prophetic in our church. The prophetic has become relevant to everyday people.

Additionally, faith increases for all of us when we see the Holy Spirit in operation. This form of prophetic ministry also helps us see that as the Father is steadfast and strong, so also is the Holy Spirit, and that His well never runs dry. Many people have had powerful encounters with the Holy Spirit, and those experiences are highlights of our lives. There is something so very wholesome about incorporating the gift of prophecy into the day-to-day lives of those we touch in our world.

Our pastors and leaders couldn't be more excited and supportive because they know their flock is getting regular injections of comfort, edification and exhortation and subsequently, the overall faith level of the church has been raised, resulting in lives being made whole, and great things being accomplished for the glory of God. In more than three years of this regular ministry, and with hundreds of people ministered to, we have never had a time where the Holy Spirit has had nothing to say. Some criticize that you can't line people up for prophecy, or that it is too conscripted to use prophecy in this way. I say, "Let the fruitfulness speak for itself!" Never in the twenty year history of having prophetic teams has our church had such "effectual, fervent" ministry in the prophetic, maintained at a constant level. There is no sign of it fizzling out!

September 2001, the day before 9/11, I was in Calgary, Alberta, presenting at a workshop on "How to build Prophetic Teams." I had just told the story of how we built and functioned through prophetic teams within our local church, and how we worked together in cooperation with our church pastor and elders. At the end of the session, a pastor got up and loudly said, "I've been waiting for twenty years to hear this, and thank God it's finally happened." The audience clapped after I finished, and the Senior Prophet hosting the meeting announced to the group that my book would be coming out soon. I was a bit flustered, as I hadn't heard God tell me to write a book, and I certainly hadn't announced that I was!

However, after countless prophecies, details arranged supernaturally, and God's clear-cut direction to me, I knew that I had to write this book. I came to realize that what we have experienced in Harvest City Church with the prophetic is *not* the norm—that very few churches have a prophetic team, and even those having prophets often don't know what to do with them. It is for all those that I write this book. For those who desire to incorporate the prophetic in their local church in a healthy way, for those who are frustrated with prophetic ministry, or maybe even a little bit frightened, for those who want to 'get it right,' but just need a little help or insight, for those who have no idea where to begin, for those who want to be obedient to the Word, and "eagerly desire the gift of prophecy" (I Corinthians 14:1); it is for all of you that I write, hoping to share some insights and encouragement that will advance the Kingdom of God, through prophecy.

WHO SHOULD READ THIS BOOK?

This is a book for pastors: who are wondering what to do with their prophetic people, or who need vision to see how the prophetic people can be an asset to their local church in a practical functioning way. It will also assist those who need some practical advice on how to go about bringing mature, uplifting prophetic voice in an appropriate manner.

This book is for prophetic people: who want to develop their gift and don't know how to make that work in the context of their church.

This book will help you begin. It will help you train and encourage the prophetic voices, and give advice on how to handle problems. It will help you organize the prophetic into a valuable resource and enjoy it as the tremendous gift to the Church that God intends it to be.

The results will be the same whether you are a pastor or a prophetic person. If you apply some of the teachings in this book, you will find a supernatural ability to work together in grace to encourage growth and development in your prophetic people. Contented prophetic people will pour prophetic comfort, edification and exhortation into the Church body. Ultimately, you will be able to work together at: "*...the full equipping of the saints...that they should do the work of ministering toward building up Christ's body (the church)."* (Ephesians 4:12).

Our goal is to have an actively functioning group of prophetic people operating in a positive, organized fashion to benefit the

Church body, by bringing the Word of the Lord to exhort, lift up, encourage and inspire.

If you are starting a prophetic team, don't be impatient with yourself or with your prophetic people. It takes time to bring order and direction, but it can be done! While we might appear to be very organized now, we started out in the loose cultural style of the seventies, and all structure that we now enjoy was built out of the discovery that doing things loosely gets a sloppy result—not to mention, discontented prophetic people and frustrated leadership! An organized, trained prophetic voice is something that you build together, with God. Don't forget: this is God's idea! The Holy Spirit will help you! And while you're at it, have some fun on the journey!

CHAPTER 1

WHY PROPHETIC TEAMS?

It was a bright, winter day when "Susan" stepped into our church youth room to receive prophetic ministry. The temperature outside was frigid, almost thirty degrees below zero with a strong wind whipping the brick exterior of the building. This was Susan's first experience with prophetic ministry.

Susan later confided: "Honestly I was not sure what to expect. I needed to hear from God. I was desperate. I consider myself a mature Christian who has a strong faith in Christ, but my circumstances were just overwhelming and I was at the end of my rope."

Susan is just one example of the many people who have received encouragement through prophetic ministry from our church and others where I am privileged to minister.

She explained, "I sat down in a chair and the small team of three people each introduced themselves. One of them held out a tiny voice recorder, about the size of a credit card, and said they would use it to record the prophetic words they were about to speak. Over the next ten minutes or so, I heard words that spoke directly into my situation. More than anything, I felt that God saw me, understood and sympathized with my situation, and was encouraging me to stand fast and persevere. There was so much that I could hardly take it all in. It was such a blessing to receive the recording a couple of days later attached to an email. As I reviewed the prophetic words, I felt renewed faith surge up from within me. My circumstances may not have changed, but I now felt I had the direction and hope that I needed to go on and realize God's eternal plan and purpose for my life."

For more than three years now, I, along with a group of trained people, host prophetic ministry opportunities to members of our congregation, their friends, family, and whoever else happens to come through our doors. In my 25 year involvement with prophetic ministry, hosting regular scheduled prophetic ministry is the most fruitful work I've ever been involved with. I feel like we are living on the edge—living the way Jesus directed by extending the Kingdom of God, and at the same time, functioning in a way that supports our church leadership, enhancing the vision of the church more than ever before.

If the Holy Spirit is as at work in your church, you will also have prophetically gifted people. Whether or not they have been acknowledged or noticed, they are there. If they have not been addressed and appropriately directed, they may be disgruntled and/or causing havoc; at the very least, they will be frustrated and feeling lost or isolated. The best way to shepherd them is to pull them into a team where they can be given guidance to help them grow and develop. At one time, about 20% of our congregation was involved in prophetic team meetings. That is likely a conservative estimate of the percentage of prophetically gifted people in any typical congregation where the Holy Spirit is at work. That is one-fifth of your congregation! So think about it. Do you want one-fifth of your members disgruntled and causing discord, or do you want that 20% of the population effectively building up and edifying the church, as a result of being taught and trained in the prophetic? What a contrast! I believe, and have confirmed through experience, that the best possible way to accomplish this is within a team structure.

Purpose of Prophetic Teams

"His intention was the perfecting and the full equipping of the saints that they might do the work of ministering toward building up Christ's body, the church...that we might arrive at really mature manhood" (Ephesians 4: 12-13).

1. Training and Development

Our primary goal in having prophetic teams is to equip and prepare those with prophetic gifting so that they function at their greatest capacity. It normally takes about twenty years for an individual operating on his or her own to develop the experience and maturity to minister effectively as a prophet, according to Graham Cooke, in his book, *Developing Your Prophetic Gifting*.[1] Cooke believes that time-frame can be reduced to twelve years with prophetic training. I have seen that theory at work in those with prophetic gifting, so whenever I hear someone in the congregation prophesying, I approach them with an invitation to the prophetic team meetings. I want to be able to work together with them to maximize their gifting, since the use of their gift definitely grows and expands through coaching.

Team ministry provides an avenue of growth for the individual—growth in ability, clarity, perspective, understanding, effectiveness...all for the purpose of blessing and encouraging the body of Christ.

A. Development—Benefits for Prophetic Individuals

Identity—Creating prophetic teams provides a venue for "prophetic gatherings." It is incredibly powerful to connect and associate with others of like mind, whether in business, personal interests, or in the body of Christ, with those similarly gifted.

Prophetically gifted persons can tend to feel somewhat different from other people, and are often misunderstood. Because of this, they often isolate themselves. That changes, however, when a 'coming together' of like-minded individuals is facilitated. Affirmation, acceptance, new understanding, and genuine enthusiasm are engendered.

Motivation—Meeting together, being part of a team, maintains momentum, giving people something to look forward to regarding their gifting. The meetings provide a specific time to focus on and develop the gift of God. The team approach provides an opportunity to sharpen one another's gifting and keep us moving forward in the prophetic. Iron does sharpen iron. Even experienced people who prophesy say they have to have opportunity to prophesy or they feel like they just dry up, and even lose confidence that they can hear from God. It is important to stay motivated!

B. Development—Benefits for the Church

Utilizing the Prophetically Gifted—From the broad team setting, you should be able to identify those individuals with the strongest prophetic gifting and have "prophets" emerging from the prophetic team.

As the team grows, you will be a greater ministry resource for the local church and beyond. Once you have this level of ministry developed, there should be evidence of fruitfulness in the lives of the church congregation. A congregation that has access to regular, ongoing prophetic ministry should see reduced levels of discouragement and depression among its members as they receive prophetic comfort, edification and exhortation.

Relationships—Considering that prophecy can be a fundamental tool used in all areas of church life, and considering the extent of the effect prophecy can potentially have, it is advisable to build good relationships between the prophetic people and church government leaders. A description of the prophetic as the "fire" and church government as the "fireplace" gives an excellent illustration of how the two can work together:

Fire burning out of control is a threat and a menace, and the fireplace structure with no fire in it is a cold, empty shell. No one wants the prophetic burning out of control, but when the prophetic is embedded in the fireplace structure, it gives warmth and a wholesome glow to everyone. In fact, the fire can burn and rage, but it is still safely contained within that structure. (Illustration taken from Chuck Porta). We want that prophetic fire to burn in our churches, blessing us all.

C. Training and Teaching—Benefits

Training time provides an opportunity to give input, thereby mentoring individuals in their gift.

Equipping Individuals—Positive teaching and training are obviously highly beneficial for advancement in any area of life; equipping people prior to ministry should be considered essential. The first time someone prophesies shouldn't be when they are on a mission or ministry trip. They should practice beforehand and gain confidence. The team setting is ideal for this. I have practical exercises built into the courses (discussed in Team Ministry sections), so that the students can experience and exercise their own prophetic gifting and become equipped for team ministry.

Coaching—Sometimes when I hear people prophesy, I know that coaching will help them prophesy better. I can hear in their prophecy when God is no longer speaking, yet the person keeps going in their own strength—or sometimes back and forth. Coaching enables people to be aware of this, and helps enable them to better identify the voice of God from their own thoughts.

Church Leaders—Attending prophetic training sessions helps church leaders have an understanding of prophetic people and prophetic gifts. A pastor or church leader may have never received training in prophecy, so attending the introductory meeting not only provides for their education, but also endorses the prophetic training going on in the church.

2. Accountability

Many prophetically gifted persons lean towards independence, especially if they aren't in a team setting when beginning to prophesy. There are inherent pitfalls when prophecy is centered on one or a few individuals, and additionally, when those who prophesy are not accountable to the leadership of a local church, there are more pitfalls. These can be avoided by utilizing a team approach. If people aren't learning and relating in a team environment, they are left to their own ideas and concepts of what prophecy should be.

There are also those who come from various denominational backgrounds, and it can sometimes be difficult to convince them that prophesying in the realm of comfort, edification and exhortation is the safe way to go—a place where you can still be a blessing but you're less subject to error. I'm working with a couple right now who have had twenty years of the theology that says prophecy is for warning and judgment, and it is difficult to swing them over to a new way of thinking.

Pastors are often nervous about the lack of prophetic accountability, so ensuring that there is proper oversight is one way of alleviating that concern. One of the reasons we have had so much success with our prophetic team is the willingness to be accountable. Even if you're not willing, you must still be held accountable.

3. Governance

Facilitate the Prophetic—In effort to ensure the growth and development of credible prophetic ministry, we have a responsibility to develop and maintain a prophetic environment. New growth is healthy. If you have a functional team, it should facilitate growth and keep both the church and prophetic persons from times of dryness and apathy. A further way in which we facilitate the prophetic is by working with a lot of outreach and offsite churches. We want to be able to offer them prophetic ministry that will be a resource for their churches. Many of those churches where we have done workshops and teaching have grown, and have now developed their own prophetic team, modeled much like ours.

Build Trust—Team structure provides a base upon which to build a solid foundation of respect and trust between church leaders and prophetic people, enabling the prophetic to flourish. Once that is established, prophetic people will feel loved and accepted and church leaders can relax, knowing the parameters for prophetic ministry are well defined and aligned with the overall vision for the local church. When there is structure in place, people feel secure. The guidelines become clear as prophetic people learn and develop at the team meetings. Church leaders feel confident that the prophetic is being shepherded, and that they can trust the prophetic team leaders to keep communication lines open should any issues or concerns arise.

Direction—a strong, developed prophetic team enables church leadership/eldership to solicit prophetic input on issues, situations and decisions.

Often in January, our Senior Prophetic Team meets with the elders, usually as part of a formal elders meeting. The Senior Team will share any prophetic words, vision or direction they have on their hearts for the church or elders concerning the upcoming year. The leadership has also invited us to give prophetic input when our church hosts regional pastors and spouses retreats.

Delegation and Order—Having a prophetic team with a designated leader provides a 'go to' person for the church leaders. Problems or suggestions can be directed to the prophetic team leader, helping to ensure consistency. Without structure, including a designated leader, two or five or ten different people may be consulted, with potential for many different answers, resulting in confusion.

4. Vision and Corporate Memory

Vision—To cast and provide ongoing vision in the prophetic for both individuals and the Church at large. At our prophetic team meeting in December or January, we ask people what is on their hearts for the New Year. We have a time of sharing which is an outlet for people to express what they have been sensing from the Holy Spirit.

Again the team setting is the perfect place for this type of discussion, and the prophetic people all get to be heard. They also get to put their word in context with the group and determine if they are in the same flow or hearing the same things. Usually there is confirmation that what they are hearing is prophetically inspired (the pieces all fit together, or line up), which is very encouraging for all.

Reflection—From time to time we reflect on significant prophetic words from the past that have been spoken to us as a Church. For example: One time it was prophesied that "Many prophets will be raised up at Harvest City Church." Other corporate prophecies that have been spoken included things like: our church will be "a house of healing" "a house of prayer," and "a house of restoration." Such prophecies are part of the overall church vision, which is reinforced by including the former with the new prophecies in our teaching. The prophetic team is given a sense of purpose as they realize they are part of the church's destiny. Furthermore, the prophetic is particularly endorsed in the Church when the pastor teaches on the prophetic direction or vision that has been identified during this time.

One time our pastor came back from a series of meetings with some networks of churches. On the same Sunday they returned, I prophesied about the harvest that was coming to our church: God was sending in the "custom combiners." That prophecy directly confirmed much of what the pastors meetings had been about, and confirmed that the topic of the meetings related specifically to our church. In keeping with that, going into the New Year, several messages were spoken preparing people to gear up for the harvest of new people coming in to the Kingdom. As a result, our church became more evangelistic in its activities and focus.

CHAPTER 2

WHAT IS PROPHECY?

From the Greek...	"propheteia," a noun which "signifies the speaking forth of the mind and counsel of God. It is the declaration of that which cannot be known by natural means. It is the forth-telling of the will of God, whether with reference to the past, the present, or the future."
Simply defined...	the Holy Spirit expressing the thoughts and desires of Christ through a human voice.
Should always be...	an extension of the gift of encouragement.

Before we delve into the main thrust of the book, which is **how to build and manage prophetic ministry in the local church**, I want to lay down some foundation for prophecy. This first chapter will serve as an overview of biblical foundation, as well as an understanding of the purpose of prophecy and prophecy basics....

Our Biblical Foundation

On His ascension, Christ gave gifts—apostles, prophets, evangelists, pastors and teachers—who are to be recognized and established in the Church world-wide and within the local church, to build up one another, strengthening the Church, and helping prepare the believers for works of ministry (Ephesians 4: 11-13).

"As each of you has received a gift, employ it for one another as it befits good trustees of God's many-sided grace. [faithful stewards of the extremely diverse powers and gifts granted to Christians by unmerited favour]" (1 Peter 4:10).

His intention was the perfecting and the full equipping of the saints [that they should do] the work of ministering toward building up Christ's body (the church) (Ephesians 4:12).

I'd like to define prophecy in everyday terms, and discuss the heart (core) purpose of prophecy in the church.

Prophecy, by more traditional definition is:

> the Declaration of that which cannot be known by natural means.
> the Forth-telling of the will of God, whether with reference to the past, the present, or the future.
> the Holy Spirit expressing the thoughts and desires of the Father and of Christ through a human voice—a mouthpiece, trumpet.

A definition that I am more comfortable with is that "prophecy is God's love letter to us." In His intense desire to communicate with us, besides His written Word, He desires to speak individually and corporately to His people. His communication with us is to be an

"I AM A LITTLE PENCIL IN THE HANDS OF A LOVING GOD WHO IS SENDING LOVE LETTERS TO THE WORLD."
–MOTHER THERESA

ongoing relationship. In Genesis 2, we read about God having daily conversation with Adam and Eve. This is a clear indication that right from the time of Creation, God's desire is to communicate with mankind. Mother Theresa sums it up so well: "I am a little pencil in the hands of a loving God who is sending love letters to the world." The prophetic person is the little pencil, that delivery person with a message from God. What a concept!

Prophecy is a supernatural gift of the Holy Spirit given to "strengthen, encourage and comfort" a believer individually, or a group of believers corporately. Graham Cooke, an established international prophet, describes prophecy as an extension of the gift of encouragement.

1 Corinthians 14:1 tells us to "...*earnestly desire and cultivate spiritual gifts, but especially that you may prophesy.*"

Being hungry for the prophetic isn't wrong; in fact God encourages us to desire spiritual gifts. I think God knows that as believers we need ongoing encouragement to keep us steady, on course and going towards our destinies. We are quick to lose vision for our lives if we don't have Holy Spirit reminders.

> **V3** "*the one who prophesies speaks to men for their up-building and constructive spiritual progress and encouragement and consolation.*"
> **V4**..."*he who prophesies edifies and improves the church and promotes growth [in Christian wisdom, piety, holiness and happiness]*" *We need prophecy in the church for our growth, wisdom, holiness and happiness.*
> **V5** "*I wish that you might all speak in tongues but more especially [I want you] to prophesy...so that the church may be edified and receive good [from it.]*"

Characteristics of Prophecy

1. *Prophecy is initiated by God*
    "For no prophecy ever originated because some man willed it [to do so—it never came by human impulse], but men spoke from God who were borne along (moved and impelled) by the Holy Spirit" (2 Peter 1:21).
    The prophet/prophetess is a *delivery* person (a vessel of communication)

2. *Prophetic gifts are for service.*

3. *Prophetic gifting is not an optional novelty.*
    Prophecy is an essential tool for effective functioning in pastoral, teaching, evangelistic or apostolic ministry.

4. *Gifts of the Spirit are not for our entertainment.*
    When used correctly, they will multiply the spiritual effectiveness of any ministry. That is why the apostle Paul exhorted the church, *"...desire earnestly spiritual gifts, but especially that you may prophesy"* (1 Corinthians 14:1b NAS).

5. *Prophecy should be increasing.* We are to expect more prophecy in the last days, according to the prophecy of Joel on the day of Pentecost:

    " 'And it shall be in the last days,' God says, 'That I will pour forth of My Spirit on all mankind; and your sons and your daughters shall prophesy, and your young men shall see visions, and your old men shall dream dreams;
    Even on My bondslaves, both men and women, I will in those days pour forth of My Spirit and they shall prophesy' " (Acts 2: 17-18 NAS).

This passage indicates that there will be *dramatic* increase in prophecy, dreams and visions in the last days.

6. ***Prophecy changed in purpose and delivery*** from the Old Testament to the New Testament.

    Once New Testament believers receive the power of the Holy Spirit, the gift of prophecy lies resident within them. They therefore have the ability to prophesy when the Spirit desires to speak, and are enabled to draw upon the gift that dwells within them.

    In Old Testament prophecy, the anointing came *upon* certain individuals. In the New Testament, the anointing dwells *within* us. The contrast is seen in the following scriptures:

Old Testament: Ezekiel 11:5 *"And the Spirit of the Lord fell upon me..."*

New Testament: Acts 2:4 *"And they were all filled with the Holy Spirit..."*

Old Testament: Isaiah 61:1 *"The Spirit of the Lord God is upon me..."*

New Testament: 1 John 2:27 *"The anointing...abides in you..."*

The same anointing that rested upon the prophets of old is now resident in the believer. Spirit-filled Christians aren't limited to relying on an external manifestation of God's Spirit. Larry Randolph, *User Friendly Prophecy*[2]

Under the Old Covenant, enquiring of the Lord and seeking guidance from the prophetic is a major function of a God-chosen person. Under the New Covenant, we obtain guidance as a direct result of the Holy Spirit being resident in our lives. The Holy Spirit resides within people, and teaches us to know the voice of God for ourselves.

Prophets today should not have the function or personality of the Old Testament. In the Old Testament prophets were feared, eccentric, intimidating and authoritarian; they brought rebuke, warning and chastisement to people.

By contrast, the New Testament prophet must exhibit the fruit of the Spirit, with grace and humility. They benefit from working in a team, and need to be an active part of the body of Christ. (Graham Cooke, *Developing Your Prophetic Gifting).*[1] Prophecy today should be based on the New Testament model, and unfortunately what we often see happening in the prophetic is that people use the Old Testament as their model, making recipients fearful and jittery. In the New Testament, with the arrival of the Holy Spirit, we see the tone of prophecy changing to become redemptive. *"...For the substance (essence) of the truth revealed by Jesus is the spirit of all prophecy..."*(Revelation 19:10). In the New Testament, encounters documented with Jesus show a gentle reminder of who He is; rarely one of rebuke and chastisement. We teach that all prophecy should lead the person towards the Lord and not away from Him.

Purpose of Prophecy

The main purpose of prophecy is to serve the body of Christ.

Prophecy is a building tool, utilized to bring blessing and encourage-ment to the body of Christ. The term "Spiritual Gifts" could give us the impression that like a gift, prophecy is only for special occasions. The Amplified Bible refers to spiritual gifts as "spiritual enablements" or "spiritual empowerments." If we view prophecy in this manner, as a building tool, it helps us understand scriptures and the intent of prophecy in a new way: 1 Corinthians 14:4 says, *"...he who prophesies edifies and improves the church and promotes growth [in Christian wisdom, piety, holiness and happiness]."* I believe that without the gift of prophecy flowing in the church, the saints individually and the

Church collectively, does not reach full maturity, nor reach the full extent of God's calling. God gave the Church the gift of prophets as one of the five-fold ministry gifts (apostles, prophets, evangelists, pastors, teachers), and it stands to reason that without prophecy, the church isn't completely balanced or whole. In the Old Testament, the building role of the prophet is seen in Ezra: "*Now the prophets, Haggai and Zechariah...prophesied to the Jews in Judah and Jerusalem in the name of the God of Israel, Whose Spirit was upon them. Then rose up Zerubbabel...and Jeshua...and began to build the house of God in Jerusalem; and with them were the prophets of God...helping them*" (Ezra 5: 1-2).

One of the roles of a prophet is exactly that, to help build the 'House of God'—being the Church—individually and collectively. Our attitude changes when we view prophecy as a tool of empowerment provided by God to expand His Kingdom. Much of the prophetic ministry is speaking Divine insight and destiny over people's lives. That usually involves conveying how God sees them very differently from the way in which they see themselves. That alone has a profound impact upon anybody! No words put together solely from the human mind could ever have a particle of the impact of the words of an all-seeing, all-knowing, completely understanding God. The prophetic, because of its completely supernatural origin, can infuse faith into people's hearts, causing them to begin to trust God and walk in the destiny He has ordained for them. Prophecy is a tool; there is impartation spiritually as Holy Spirit inspired words are deposited into the person's heart.

I've experienced this encouragement personally in a way I will never forget: My husband and I had been believers in a church for about five years when the leadership had to be forcibly removed because of a moral failure. It seemed like our vision, destiny and purpose were dying with that situation. Additionally, the church was left with a 1.8 million dollar debt. Obviously we were at a very low point in our lives—we were confused, disappointed, angry and disillusioned. Many of our friends just left and bombed out. At this time a prophet friend came to that church and said to my husband, "How are you, you mighty man of God?" With us feeling so low and humiliated, that simple prophetic word breathed life into our very spirits! That was almost thirty years ago, and I still cannot tell the story without tears coming to my eyes. That prophetic word, along with God's grace, carried us through those grim times. This encouragement helped us to soldier on to reach a higher level of maturity in our Christian walk.

CHAPTER 3

HOW TO BUILD
A PROPHETIC TEAM

Sometimes, people feel like they need to be an expert, or at least tremendously prophetically gifted in order to start a team. If you are, that's great, but it is not a requirement—God is bigger than our inadequacies. Starting a team does require faith, however—faith that God wants to enlarge us as individuals, and as a church. I believe that any person who has leadership qualities and even a small amount of prophetic gifting can be an effective team leader. Often, a pastor whose main gift is not even prophecy will be the one to start a team.

A successful team will be focused on the principle of service. It must be a real team effort and not centred upon any single person or elite group of so-called prophets. Sometimes, prophetic people can be

A SUCCESSFUL TEAM WILL BE FOCUSED ON THE PRINCIPLE OF SERVICE.

strong and/or unique individuals, and not easy to corral. Because of this, the idea of starting and leading a team may seem daunting, or a team dismantles soon after starting out. The key to having a successful team is to emphasize, right from day one, that prophecy is a group effort, and not a building up of any individual person's ministry. This is the life of the team—serving.

Getting Started

1. Make the Decision

You may not have complete direction or see the whole picture, but if you make the decision to start, the rest will fall into place. There is a temptation to want the whole vision right from the beginning.

Don't be afraid to start small and simple. God leads one step at a time and often only reveals the next step just before you take it.

2. Pray

Sometimes the obvious gets overlooked! Prophecy is God's gift to us— He wants us to be operating in this gift. We need to *ask* for direction— He will be sure to provide it!

3. Include the Youth!

We see a prophetic mantle falling upon people earlier in life. When there are second, third and fourth generation kids in a congregation, you can be assured that they have absorbed a lot of knowledge and skills (almost by osmosis) in the environment where they have grown up. Younger people have a greater tendency to see and hear things as they are, since they are not able to put everything through a long grid of personal experience. Because of this, it's sometimes easier for them to see and hear more clearly. If I want to get a perspective on advice that comes from the Senior Team, I will often ask my kids. They have real clarity in Kingdom vision, and they are now just in their twenties!

4. Identify the person with a call to lead

Initially, it may be the pastor starting and leading the group, but he or she should be on the look-out for one who is called to lead. This person is likely a diamond in the rough whose gifting is not fully developed, but demonstrates genuine vision and passion. In fact, it's quite likely that person initially does have an undeveloped gifting. (People identi-fied the gift in me long before I actually became a leader.) If the person is solid, loyal and teachable, they will grow into the task of leading while counting on the pastoral team as advisors.

5. Have a long term vision

Sometimes people are impatient, expecting others to gain prophetic maturity overnight. It is valuable to recognize from the outset that strong prophetic ministry takes time to build. Training in the prophetic is an ongoing process and it takes time to bear fruit, but once people gain their confidence, the prophetic really ignites.

6. Establish regular team meetings

People need consistency to develop in their gifting. Use the team meetings as an opportunity to address issues specific to prophetic people. For example:

a) Reminders: to consider the time constraints of an event while prophesying, to keep prophecy redemptive and restorative, to use appropriate tone and ensure clarity when giving a prophetic word.

b) Prophetic people need to connect and relate with one another. Help them to see the broader picture: "You're not the only one…who feels this way/ thinks this way."

c) Discuss common issues such as insecurity, intimidation, the "Am I hearing from God or not?" question.

d) Reign in the mavericks. If people are too independent to work within a team setting, they usually are too independent to be useful in our prophetic environment, even though they may have a strong gift. Test them to see if they will yoke themselves to a team. (They may simply lack understanding of this concept, depending on their background experience.) This sounds really basic; however we have had a few mavericks over the years.

What usually happens is: they start coming to the team meetings and attract a lot of attention, but eventually it becomes
apparent that their focus is on their own ministry and not on
the team. They are often too set in their ways, and feel stifled by
the team setting—wanting to be out there on their own, just
them and God. While we want to give them time to get used to
the idea of working within a team, we also expect them to
mature, accept teaching, and learn to work together with the
group.

7. Establish criteria

a) At first, people may be selected to join based on evidence of
gifting or by invitation only. As you grow, you may ask for a rec-
ommendation from a home group leader, youth pastor, elder
etc. You can open it up once the foundation of the team is established. Initially, when we began our first team, we only had
people with an identified gifting come by invitation. However,
now that the teams have been established, anyone can attend
introductory team meetings. Team members should be active in
the church.

b) It is important to avoid an "elitist" attitude or a focus on gifting
alone. The prophetic ministry is a serving ministry, not different
from the janitor called to serve and clean the church building.
We don't elevate the prophet above other ministries. Ideally
people should be attending the church for six months before
they start coming to team meetings in order to give them a
chance to get a feeling for the vision and ministry focus of the
church (the church DNA). Once they have that, it's then easier
for them to put the prophetic into perspective, and see how it
fits into the overall operation of the church. People who come
in from other churches may or may not adapt to another
church. Personally, I feel I've wasted a lot of time with some

people who are ultimately waiting for you to change to their way of doing things. In the end, these type of people move on to another church. This is one reason why it is important that team members be established in the church first.

c) Minister in pairs—partner a more experienced person with a novice. We follow this guideline whether we are at a prophetic team meeting or doing public ministry; it's such a good safeguard! The novice can rely on the Intermediate or Senior Prophetic person to take the lead, and so feels less pressure to generate words beyond those received from the Holy Spirit. People receiving ministry tend to hear things through their own personal filters, which can lead to misunderstanding. Having people prophesy in pairs creates accountability and transparency.

8. Recognize the shepherding role in oversight of the prophetic team

a) We're interested in the whole person, not just their gifting. Character development is part of the process.

b) Prophetic people:

➤ Need encouragement.
➤ Need teaching.
➤ Need balance and adjustment. Sometimes they need a referral for counseling to help them deal with their issues. Even if the person is prophetically very gifted, there is a time where they have to deal with their inner issues, or those un-dealt with issues will hinder their ministry.

Work with the individuals' home group leaders or youth pastor as the need arises.

9. Look for growth opportunities

Identify individuals who can help teach, lead meetings, or participate in public ministry. Find resources that will develop your team: DVDs, websites, books, teaching material—over time establish a resource library.

10. Be flexible

Don't interpret irregular attendance as lack of commitment. Recognize that team members have career, home and/or church responsibilities. Allow introductory and intermediate members to develop at their own pace. Some people have stayed in the introductory group for two or three years in a row. Some leave for a period of time and come back later. Because of the pace of life and competing demands on people's time, it may take two or three years to get the complete set of introductory teachings.

11. Work with the church leaders

The team leader is under the authority of the church leadership, and needs to be supported by the pastor and elders. I give occasional reports to the elders to keep them up-to-date on the prophetic ministry. Sometimes a pastor or elder will attend a Senior Team meeting just to see what's happening, what we're planning or talking about. It's an encouragement and an endorsement of their support for us. This approach builds strength, security and unity, and our ongoing relationship allows the prophetic to flow freely in our church within an atmosphere of mutual trust and respect.

12. Have prophetic vision for the individual, as well as for the team

As the team develops, those with strong prophetic mantles should emerge. The team setting helps to identify the flavour of someone's prophetic gifting.

For example: prophetic intercessor, prophetic evangelist, prophetic teacher, prophetic counselor (those with strong words of wisdom).

13. Create opportunity

There is a need for prophetic people to prophesy and to grow in their gifting. The practical activities at every team meeting have been invaluable for developing gifting and confidence. Look for opportunities to include team members in public prophetic ministry. Example: baptisms, prayer team ministry.

a) Model your message.

b) Give deference to others in prophetic ministry.

c) Offer the microphone to those whom you think may have a word.

d) Keep prophecy sharp. Avoid vague, repetitive or prophetic words that do not have a clear point.

e) Don't steal the limelight. Build up the team. Use 'us' and 'we' versus 'I' and 'me'. Set an example of service to individuals and the church. Service is the best antidote to a 'prima donna' mentality. Serving is what we're called to do!

Overview of Prophetic Teams

For the past fifteen years, our prophetic ministry has been structured with three teams: the Introductory, Intermediate, and Senior Teams. I coordinate all three, and am accountable to the eldership team. People new to the prophetic are encouraged to attend monthly introductory team meetings where they receive teaching and practical foundation regarding the prophetic culture of our church. Those who are strongly prophetic continue on to the Intermediate meetings. The decision to attend is by choice, but if anyone prophesies publicly in the church, I or other leaders suggest that they attend prophetic meetings. Both the Introductory and Intermediate meetings are held the same night, and the groups are separated for the teaching and the practical exercise. Details pertaining to each team are provided in the following sections. The Senior Team functions as the prophetic governance; these members are asked to join in consultation with the eldership team. One does not move onto the Senior Team by graduating from the intermediate class—this is also discussed more fully in the team sections.

Practical Steps in Starting a Prophetic Team

Beforehand

> ➤ Announce about three weeks ahead of time you are starting a prophetic team for interested people.
> ➤ Provide the contact person's name and phone number/email for those who want to discuss or ask questions ahead of time. (Many people don't know if they are 'intercessory' or prophetic.)
> ➤ Put the meeting information on your church website or in the bulletin.
> ➤ At the first meeting, have a sign-in contact sheet with phone numbers and email addresses.
> ➤ Appoint an assistant who will keep attendance sheets and set up the contact lists.
> ➤ Contact people 1 weeks before the meeting as a reminder. Do that for every meeting. (Mass email works well.)

The Meeting

> ➤ Keep meetings to about two hours in length.
> ➤ Start with worship, announce upcoming events.
>   Open a meeting sometimes with corporate prophecy.
>   Include a testimony from time to time.
> ➤ Have a teaching time for about 45 minutes, and then start a practical activity.
> ➤ Don't fall into the temptation of just teaching; the success of the team comes from the practical activity.

➢ Encourage people that they are on the right track. The leader should try to circulate while the activity is going on. Give individual attention to ones who are floundering with the activity.

➢ Pull the group together at the end of the meeting to review the prophetic exercises. Stay positive in the sharing times. Don't embarrass or intimidate anyone with your comments.

➢ Allow time at the end of the meeting to circulate to people "hanging around" and give them one-on-one attention.

➢ Let them share personal experiences or ask questions.

➢ If someone wants an in-depth conversation, set up a coffee time with them. Don't let the meeting night go on and on, or you will lose people over time. They should be able to have a planned ending time.

➢ Let them know when the next meeting will be.

Afterward

➢ Try to talk with people at times other than the meeting in order to build a relationship with them.

➢ Contact people 1½ weeks before the next scheduled meeting to remind them.

CHAPTER 4

THE INTRODUCTORY TEAM

The purpose of an introductory team is to get people to actively grow and develop in their gifting, enabling them to be effective in ministering to the body of Christ and eventually the market-place (the world) around them. Here they can learn the foundations of prophecy and develop the technique of prophesying. Technique is defined as skill in a particular practical art or applied science, according to a set of rules or regulations.

People with prophetic gifting need to train and develop towards maturity. There is a pervasive attitude that if individuals have a true prophetic gift, it will develop itself over time. That may be true in exceptional individuals but for most, proper training and development will help avoid some of the following problems:

> ➢ Inappropriate prophetic style—too long, harsh tone, disconnected thoughts, or following an Old Testament model.
> ➢ Inaccurate prophecy—blending thoughts, ideas or words that originate from the person giving the prophecy together with the message that God wants to communicate.
> ➢ Using distracting mannerisms.
> ➢ Blurting out prophecy at inappropriate times. Sometimes when people are new, they can overwhelm others with a barrage of prophecy, becoming so focused on what they are saying that they are oblivious to their surroundings. One pastor's wife told me she was mistrustful of prophecy for years, as earlier in

her life a prophetic person came up to her and "attacked" her with prophecy.

➤ Prophesying judgement or warnings. Having a foundation of incorrect doctrine, believing that the main purpose of prophecy is warning and judgement. Use of judgemental words such as "you have a root of bitterness," or "you are sick because of unforgiveness," which should not be given.

Benefits of Having an Introductory Team

1. *Provides people with an opportunity*, within a nonthreatening environment, to find out whether or not they have a prophetic gift. Sometimes people find out that what they thought was a prophetic gift turns out to be more of an intercessory gifting, and that their calling is to pray and intercede for others.

2. *Allows people to receive foundational* Biblical teaching on the prophetic.

3. *Gives an opportunity for mentoring.* As appropriate, members of the Senior Team are encouraged to teach and work with the Introductory group, becoming mentors to them. This is beneficial for both.

4. *Provides opportunity for people to get to know your church's prophetic DNA.* I like to get people into prophetic team meetings because there is so much you can teach them about your prophetic heartbeat and your church culture of the prophetic.

5. *Provides understanding that gifting must be developed within guidelines.* This helps build credibility for the prophetic, and creates the required trust for pastors and leaders to release prophetic ministry into the ecosystem of the local church.

a) Provides an opportunity to learn prophetic etiquette and generally accepted practices.

b) Individuals begin to understand that we are accountable for the prophetic words we deliver. Anytime we prophesy over someone, we always have another person (preferably a leader) paired with one who is learning.

c) Giving deference to others is taught and modelled; we teach that we don't have to prophesy every time we are given the opportunity, but can make room for others.
"Be devoted to one another in brotherly love; give preference to one another in honour" (Romans 12:10).

d) Allows for feedback and evaluation of prophecy. In prophetic training, we ensure that prophecy is evaluated. *"Let two or three prophets speak, and let the others pass judgement"* (1Corinthians 14:29 NAS). Within the group we can learn from each other's mistakes, ask questions, and receive further instruction from Senior Team members.

WE WANT TO GIVE DEFERENCE TO OTHERS; THAT WE DON'T HAVE TO PROPHESY EVERY TIME WE ARE GIVEN THE OPPORTUNITY, BUT CAN MAKE ROOM FOR OTHERS.

6. ***Prophetic ability can be developed.*** The prophetic person can go from an occasional use of the gift to a prophetic ministry. I often use team meetings to exhort people to stir up their gift, to encourage them to prophecy. Beginners are encouraged to give words at prayer meetings or pre-service prayer times. It's sad to say, but too many dismiss those opportunities as not being adequate for their gifting and wait to make all their mistakes in

a big public setting, or alternatively, never prophesy at all because they've never stepped out, allowing their confidence to be built.

Participation

At least once during introductory training I set up a mini-service where we have half an hour or so of worship, then encourage people to begin to step out in prophecy. We have a microphone set up, and they have to use an orderly pattern of one person following the other giving their word. It happens time after time that we see a theme, as each person presents their piece of the puzzle; then the whole picture unfolds. It helps them to see that every single part is important—that the Holy Spirit really is in control! They are so much more confident knowing they've received and given prophecy. It almost doesn't matter what is prophesied (because the confidence to trust in God is what is important). I use almost anything they speak out prophetically and work with it. Most of the time you can pull out a theme to work with, and that really builds confidence.

Sometimes, even when you know the person is prophetic they can have some 'off the wall' prophecies. One time we were working on an exercise, and one of the people said they had received a real prayer burden for John Travolta (well known for his Scientology beliefs). Well, I guess that could be true, but it wasn't all that relevant to the meeting. Instead of dismissing it, I used it as a teaching opportunity to point out that God can use these times in His presence to put people on our hearts and minds for prayer and intercession. Whoever is leading the meeting must be sensitive, and not embarrass nor discourage the free flow of the prophetic—at least the person stepped out and tried! I also like people to connect at prophetic team meetings so they can share common struggles and encourage each other.

Teaching the Technique of Prophecy that Edifies

1. Developing a trained ear

It's vital that brand-new prophetic people learn to hear the difference between someone just starting to prophesy, and those who are experienced. I teach that prophecy is a mixture of God and self, and that as we grow in the gift we should be hearing more of God and less of self. I want them to train their ears so they can recognize the difference. Graham Cooke uses an illustration with a graph as follows.

Swimming Pool Depth of Ministry[2]

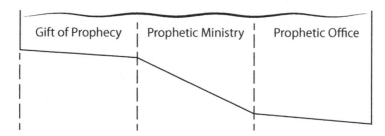

You can see that as we move deeper, becoming a mature, seasoned prophet, there should be more of God speaking and less of self.

2. Learning respectful behaviour

I believe it is important for the introductory group to respect those that have a developed gift, and pay attention in order to identify what can be learned from them. When someone is prophesying, it's important for the others who have prophetic gifting to focus and really listen to what's being said instead of trying to concentrate on hearing a word from God themselves. We are not competing with one another, rather we are trying to catch the theme of what God wants to communicate, and allow the prophetic to give voice through us in an orderly manner. It might sound surprising that respectful behaviour has to be addressed, but I find increasingly that people need to be taught prophetic etiquette.

3. Prophesy in teams, not individually

We teach the introductory team to prophesy in groups of two or three. Right from the first exercise they are indirectly learning that they have to be accountable with their words. The groups are made up entirely of novices to reduce any "performance anxiety." Since they are grouped with other novices, it is very nonthreatening. As they listen to one another prophesy, they are also getting an ear tuned to hear what is the 'God part' of the prophecy and what was the 'self part' of prophecy. We conduct an exercise where they are required to judge the word and identify what is the God or self part. Again, this is non-threatening and not personal, as we know and help them recognize that anyone new to prophecy will initially have a mixture. We also teach that as we prophesy in groups, often we each get a piece of the puzzle to give. That piece on its own might not have a lot of meaning but as the words are put together, it is evident that God is orchestrating a complete message.

4. Be aware of "mind battles"

One battle we must fight is taking the words God gives us, and attempting to put them through our own framework so that they make sense to us. However, something that seems incomplete to us is usually very relevant to the receiver—a phrase or a picture—will resonate with the receiver. Before I understood this, I wasted a lot of time trying to manage the prophetic by putting words in order or shaping the message.

I have been in situations where I was so immersed in the prophetic that I had no choice but speak exactly what I'd received. Because I had to move so fast, it was the only thing I could do. Those experiences taught me that it's better just to give it straight, and count on God's grace to cover me.

5. Respect for the receiver

I always teach people they need to be considerate toward the people to whom they are ministering. If God reveals to us something negative, or an area of sin, we must prophesy using words and terminology that are redemptive. What good would it do to expose an area of sin or weakness and leave the person feeling condemned? Does God ever do that? He always leads people towards Himself. Considering that, we always want to prophesy hope, even in difficult areas, and speak to people about their way of escape.

6. Teach people not to have verbal overload

People beginning in the prophetic often get a "lot of information." It seems that when God opens the prophetic gate, there can be a flood of dreams, visions, words of knowledge, and the person can become overwhelmed.

PEOPLE BEGINNING IN THE PROPHETIC OFTEN GET A "LOT OF INFORMATION."

When that happens:

a) First, they have to calm down. Remind them that God is not going anywhere—there is no need to panic, and that the prophetic gift is just being confirmed in the person's life.

b) Now the growth and development comes in—the time when they have to learn what to do with the information. Most beginners feel that they have to share everything they get with someone. Often, they contact me, initially wanting an ongoing relationship whereby I would analyze everything that's going on. First of all, I don't have time to listen to several people's dreams, visions or whatever, but even if I did, I wouldn't. The prophetic person needs to grow and develop a confidence in their own ability to hear from God.

If they come to me with a dream, warning or whatever, I'll ask them:

- Have they have written it down?
- If so, have they prayed about what God would have them do with the information?
- Do they think it might be a way God is speaking to them to pray and intercede for that person?

I would direct them to do these things, and then see if they still think God wants them to speak to the person they have on their heart. Ninety-nine percent of the time, after they have prayed about the situation, they don't feel the need to go directly to the person in the dream. I then encourage them to write a card, or go alongside that person and tell them God had placed them on their heart and that they've been praying for them—without going into the details.

That may be the end of their assignment, so they learn there is a process in place, and not every word given to them requires individual or public declaration.

If they have had a dream that is recurring or they think it's prophetically significant for the church or a certain ministry area, I'll have them write the dream out for discussion at the next Senior Team meeting, and provide them with feedback at that time. I don't want to discourage people beginning in prophetic revelation, but they need to understand that it must be put in context, and is often a message for intercessory prayer.

7. Have mentoring opportunities outside the meetings.

As a leader in the prophetic, it is natural that a lot of people in the group want to be my friends so we can talk "prophetic talk" all the time. I really like the fact that within a team setting they can find the camaraderie they desire, and nurture each other to grow and develop. They have time for each other. I see my role as an overseer; therefore my role requires that

I take extra personal time with those evidencing strong gifting along with a desire to serve. At one time, I tried to meet for coffee with most of the women on the prophetic team, but as we have grown, my time has to go into organizing and coordinating all that is going on in the prophetic. It is therefore essential that people form these relationships amongst themselves. I also try to assign the Senior Team members to follow up and connect with people from the other teams.

8. Don't be afraid to have fun in the meetings!

A bond is created as we laugh together and share stories of our victories and defeats. Teach people to be real and vulnerable, not to have a facade of holiness or spirituality.

Indicators for Asking People to Join the Team

> **Evidence**: They are already prophesying.
> **Referral**: Other leaders will recommend they come to the classes.
> **Holy Spirit**: Often when I'm around people, I will sense the Holy Spirit telling me the person is prophetic. I usually wait to see if I sense it another time or two when I'm around that person. Sometimes, upon invitation, the person responds immediately and takes advantage of the opportunity being offered for training. Other times the person will acknowledge that they are prophetic, but based on past unpleasant experiences they have squelched the gift and don't want to get involved. I keep encouraging those people to give it another try. One woman only just began coming to the team meetings after three years of personal encouragement to come. I gave her the victory sign as I saw her come into the back of the room.
> **Direct Enquiry**: People may approach me with questions about prophecy. This is a good indicator of having a prophetic gift.
> **General Invitation**: Make announcements in the church bulletin and in church services about prophetic teams and

prophetic ministry so that those interested may enquire. If possible, speak in the church at least once per year to provide basic understanding of what prophecy is, and to invite new people to the Introductory Meeting.

Introductory Group General Guidelines

People showing any prophetic gifting are encouraged to come to Introductory Team meetings, including those who think they may be prophetic, and those who are interested in learning about the prophetic in order to assist them in the leadership of others. Example: Small group/Home group leaders.

We are pretty open about who can attend this group; if you are considered part of the Church body, you can come! Initially, when we started prophetic teams, we were much more guarded with who could be included in the group, but as the groups have expanded and we have become more confident in our leadership we have been able to have a more "open door" policy. We actually encourage people to come for some introductory classes because we believe that "*you may all prophesy*" (1 Corinthians 14:31). It is an asset to the body of Christ if everyone learns to step out in their gifting.

When we are asked if people can invite their friends from other churches, we request that they obtain permission from their pastor first. We want to maintain good inter-church relationships, and this is a good open communication policy. If someone is from another church where they aren't allowed to prophesy, and there is no room for growth in prophecy, I tell them they will only be more frustrated if they develop their gift at a team meeting but are never given opportunity to prophesy. In that case, it may be better not to attend for the time being. They should certainly seek the instruction of the Lord concerning such a matter.

We keep a flexible attitude towards attendance at the meetings. The Introductory training is scheduled monthly between September and May each year. Because people are busy with their ministry and life involvements, it's not unusual for a person to attend the introductory group for a two year period just to take in all the classes. We are quite firm on people completing the Introductory classes before moving on to the Intermediate team. If someone is a really a novice regarding spiritual matters and spiritual gifts, they will often decide themselves that they want to repeat the Introductory course.

Our goal is to have people feel comfortable in their gift and develop a heart for the prophetic. For example, we don't treat the Intermediate group as something to strive for, or evidence that someone has "arrived," and going through the groups is not a stepping stone to the Senior Team. The Senior Team is different in that it also operates in a governmental role, and that is not for all team members. Operating in such a capacity requires particular gifting and/or skills that certain individuals possess; therefore, being part of that group is invitational—confirmed by an elder.

WE DON'T TREAT WORDS GIVEN AT AN INTRODUCTORY MEETING ON THE SAME LEVEL AS THOSE GIVEN BY A PROPHET.

The atmosphere we strive to achieve in the Prophetic Team meetings is one where people feel safe enough to step out in their gifting, and unafraid to make a mistake. We ensure that the practical activity time makes allowance for mistakes; we don't treat words given at an Introductory meeting on the same level as those given by a prophet. We use humour and strive to help the prophetic people "lighten up."

While I was teaching recently, I could hear this funny moaning sound. One of the people who attend the group is blind, and I slowly realized her Seeing Eye dog was snoring. I tried to ignore him, even though I could hear snickers from the group. Finally his owner accidentally knocked a book off the table. The book, entitled *Is This the End of the World*, landed on the dog's head, and gave him a start. We all had a chuckle. It's good to keep things on the lighter side when you can.

One of the practical activities we use is to blindfold three people sitting in chairs. We sit someone in a chair behind the three in chairs, and we have great fun as they prophesy; the prophecies will often hit on some personality quirk or behavior the receiver has. Our former pastor did this activity once and was described as "being on a flying trapeze, swinging from one rope to another." It was very comical picturing him wearing the spandex suits known to trapeze artists.

I find that most prophetic people, particularly Canadians, are really shy with their gift. Getting out each prophecy can be a battle, and fear is the enemy: fear of making mistakes, fear of being judged and intimidation.

Just coming to the meetings and discovering that these are common battles is a big relief to many of them. The group setting provides support and encouragement to help overcome these obstacles.

The Introductory Group creates a forum to help the leaders determine the type and level of gifting each person has, and then advises each person accordingly. Some may be encouraged to join a character building group to deal with inner issues before continuing on to the Intermediate level. Others might be advised they would better fit in an intercessory prayer or other group that is more suitable to their gifting.

CHAPTER 5

THE INTERMEDIATE TEAM

Benefits of Having an Intermediate Team

1. *Provides the opportunity for interaction*, support and development of prophetic gifting. There is great strength in having connection with other prophetic people; it meets a critical need of relating to others like-minded, and allows for the sharing of both victories and failures.

2. *Provides more opportunity for team leaders to build relationships* with individuals in the group. Having relationship allows leaders to speak more directly into peoples' lives.

3. *Provides opportunity for training and development*, which helps people develop greater prophetic "flow." Training at this level builds on the foundation laid during the introductory course.

4. *The teaching is deeper*, and the level of responsibility and accountability increases.

5. *Allows team leaders to identify levels of gifting* in people so that opportunities can be offered to those with evidence of stronger or developed gifting. Eventually those that have a calling of a "prophet" can be identified.

6. ***Evidence of leadership ability is uncovered.*** When leaders emerge, they can then be called upon to function/serve in a greater capacity. For example, ask them to help with administrative duties for the meetings.

7. ***Provides an appropriate time and place to address any issues*** originating from the church setting. Example: the elders thought there wasn't enough prophecy taking place when people were being baptized—they wanted me to encourage the Intermediate Team to "stir up their gift."

The Format

We have maintained a consistent format over the years, and it has proven constructive. We have a teaching time, followed by an activity. Approximately half of the meeting is teaching, the other half activity. Originally, we had about thirty minutes of worship and our meetings easily went until 10:00 p.m. (I would often be delayed talking to team members, and not arrive home until 11:00). Now we start at 7:30, have two or three worship songs (about ten minutes) and our evening of teaching and activity sessions are over by about 9:15. Adopting a timed structure such as this works well for everyone. People are more likely to come regularly if the meeting is timely and structured, and they can expect to be finished at a reasonable time—consistently.

How Often Do We Meet?

Usually once per month, however, other church activities must be considered. It is preferable to have a reasonable number of meetings that all may attend. Eight to ten sessions per year is ideal, and allows for maximum accomplishment.

What Do We Teach?

We initially used the prophetic courses developed by Bill Hamon *Prophetic 101 and Prophetic 202*[3]—adapted for our environment, including some of our own activities.

Some of the useful books we've studied include:

> *You May All Prophesy* by Steve Thompson [4] (highly recommended for prophecy basics)
> *Can you hear me?* by Brad Jersak[5]
> *Foundations of Prophecy and Developing a Supernatural Lifestyle* by Graham Cooke[6]
> *Developing a Supernatural Lifestyle* by Kris Vallotton[7]

We are constantly working on varying the theme and/or bringing in different speakers for teaching. For example, we teach on Prophetic Evangelism. Additionally, we utilize various ministry opportunities to strengthen and develop the team. (See Chapter 14.)

Seek to keep the group relevant and outwardly focused in terms of ministry. Many people have been in the group for several years now, so they have likely prophesied over each other several times. Inviting different people in to be prophesied over helps mix things up, provides greater prophetic challenge, and heightens the enthusiasm of the group.

KEEP THE GROUP RELEVANT AND OUTWARDLY FOCUSED

It's important to offer a variety of teaching/activities or we become stale, unmotivated and dull!

Technique

Prophetic flow: As people have opportunity to minister, they gain confidence to step out in the prophetic, requiring more feedback on their technique. It takes time to develop a "prophetic flow." When people start out prophesying, they get words, a sentence, or a picture. It takes time and practical experience to develop the technique of being able to speak those words or pictures while new words are coming. While they are learning, their words can be choppy, or there may be long pauses in their message. It is ideal to minister in a team setting so that people can have the time to learn technique. This is how the team approach works: One person may see a picture, and prophesy just that. Another person may have the interpretation. In this way, the pressure is off that person with the picture to try to "come up with" more than what has been given to them. People should prophesy slowly and clearly enough so that they can be heard. We ask people to guard against getting directive. (Refer to end of chapter for tips on prophesying.)

Prophesying from notes: When a prophetic person knows in advance that they will be prophesying, they may jot down notes. I still do that from time to time, especially if I'm involved in a whole weekend of ministry; things may come to me as I glance over at a person, but there may not be opportunity to prophesy right that minute. I write it down. If I have a word over a church, I often get some impressions ahead of the ministry time. When prophesying from notes, however, it's best to use them as a spring board. Just reading notes doesn't have the same impact or strength in anointing as speaking out the prophecy.

Taking risks: As people grow and develop established prophetic ministries, they can begin to take risks in prophesying more of what they are hearing. We work alongside people and normally caution them not to go beyond the level of comfort, edification and exhortation. If, however, they become established prophetically, and are together in a situation with a Senior prophetic person, they may get more directional and share words of knowledge. It's a dicey area, though. Accuracy is important—inaccuracy has the potential for serious results in the lives of those you are ministering to. When they get it right, everyone applauds, but if it's 'off,' it has to be discussed as a learning opportunity with the prophetic person. It's usually wise to counsel the person who has received the prophecy in order to clarify anything that may have been 'off' or inaccurate. This will assist the person learning to prophesy, and will help the receiver to put the word in the appropriate perspective.

Being flexible in our ministry style: Prophetic people shouldn't get so set in one style of ministering that they can't bend or be flexible beyond that. For example: I find it much easier to prophesy with my eyes shut, but there are times, especially when you're talking to a person who does not know God / Jesus personally, that you need to look them in the eye and speak to them. If you don't, they'll think you're weird, and quite likely have a hard time receiving from you.

There are settings in which we prophesy where it may be okay to speak loudly and pray in tongues, and other settings where there is not the same liberty. I was recently participating in a conservative church's women's night, and was able to minister to women by *praying* prophetically. It didn't hinder my gifting, and I could still be respectful of their way of doing things. We should have the maturity to be sensitive to the type of group or individuals we are addressing. Prophesy doesn't have to 'look' a particular way—we shouldn't be so rigid in how we do things that we limit the field in which God can use us.

Recently I was ministering with a team in a church that had 75% of the Sunday service filled with new believers. The pastor knew we had a prophetic word to give to the congregation regarding the future direction of the church. I put him at ease when I told him I could share the prophetic word just by explaining to the congregation that as we had been in their city over the last two days, God had been showing us some things about their church. There was no problem with people hearing and understanding the prophetic word as I spoke it using everyday conversation. It didn't diminish the word by giving it in an unprophetic-like style.

Ministry Opportunities for the Intermediate Team

While team meetings are great, and highly valuable for teaching, practice, and interaction between those like-minded, what must remain at the forefront is that the ultimate goal of prophecy is ministering to people. Do not allow your teams to become totally inward focused!

Encourage people to use their gift in different settings. Examples:

> ➤ Encourage the people to take advantage of an upcoming "worship night" or prayer meeting in the church by preparing themselves and expecting to prophesy.

> ➤ Invite ministries within the church that are facing challenges (like needing more workers). Encourage them with prophetic words from God.

> ➤ Send out members to minister with other ministries, such as Healing Rooms or inner healing ministries.

> ➤ Minister to support groups.

> ➤ Bring in leaders from other churches, city ministries, or organizations for an evening to prophesy over them and build them up.

> ➤ Invite specific ministry groups from other churches and prophesy over them.

> ➤ Invite members of the introductory team to receive prophetic ministry.

> ➤ Prophecy at Water Baptisms. What a great opportunity to exercise their gift and be a blessing to the people being baptized! Most are new converts, so they have no great expecta-

tions about the prophecy received. They are just blessed by the encouragement. I usually have a Senior prophetic person overseeing the ministry, but we try to involve as many intermediate level people as possible.

➤ Be involved in the 'between-service' ministry (discussed in Chapter 15). This is the absolute best way to have prophetic people develop their gift. As they minister on a regular basis, they can concentrate on hearing God's voice and develop a well-balanced style of prophetic delivery.

We don't want people getting stagnant in their gift; they must have practical opportunities. So many ministries are looking for people willing to use their gifting and to serve—make the most of a great match!

Final Thoughts about the Intermediate Team

It is always a challenge to come up with ongoing interesting teaching topics for the intermediate team. We keep variety by alternating book studies with teachings developed in-house, utilizing a variety of teachers for the sessions—usually Senior Team members or visiting ministry.

While this time to teach and learn is necessary, perhaps even more important is the opportunity to keep the prophetic people connected, and work on developing their gift. It's also the time that we get to make any adjustments or emphasize certain things in the practice of the prophetic. Team meetings are a significant time just for prophetic people, so that we can speak directly and specifically to their needs.

CHAPTER 6

THE SENIOR TEAM

Definition

The prophetic teams are not a hierarchy, with membership on the Senior Team achieved by going through the Introductory and Intermediate courses. The Senior Team is governmental—we work with the pastor and elders to oversee prophetic ministry in the church, and are a support and resource to the eldership team. For a pastoral team, this is a huge bonus. Issues that come up regarding the prophetic, including any correction or adjustment needed in individual lives, are dealt with by the Senior Team, working in cooperation with the pastor or elders as needed. This takes a tremendous amount of pressure off the pastors/elders, and places initial responsibility with those familiar with the issues. Furthermore, it creates opportunity for growth and development of leadership skills in those ready to take on such tasks.

Why we started

The Senior Team was based on an identified need, like most other processes and structures we have in place. While the Introductory and Intermediate teams were fairly well established, my husband made the observation that I had become the point person for all the prophetic input, as well as problems resulting from the prophetic. From his objective vantage point, he could see and recommend that when decisions are being made regarding an individual or a situation, it is better to have a group be accountable for such leadership responsibilities.

The key to successfully taking on such responsibilities is to establish good working relationships with the church leadership. I cannot see this model working any other way—there has to be a genuine trust between the prophetic leaders and the church pastoral/leadership team.

A Senior Team structure has several advantages:

➢ Many perspectives are presented, not just one single leader's perspective.

➢ Decisions made concerning prophetic people don't seem so personal. It is more difficult for an individual to get offended with an entire group, as opposed to just one person.

➢ Shared responsibilities of decision making reduces the burden on any one leader. Initially I approached the elders, asking them to identify those of the prophetic people whom they felt should be part of the Senior Team. At the same time, I made my own selection list. The elders' lists coincided with mine, and those people were selected for the team. At the time, it was a simple and general request to help me with the oversight of the prophetic; later on we established some of the goals and purposes of the team. The Senior Team has been functioning in an established capacity for some time now, and it seems to me, has become a part of who we are, rather than how we are functioning.

Benefits of Having a Senior Team

A. Benefits for the Pastor

Shepherding and Pastoring of the overall prophetic in the church is handled by the Senior Team. Once the team is working effectively, the burden of overseeing the prophetic ministry and prophetic people should be lifted off the pastoral staff. When there is a prophetic person or issue to deal with, the call comes to me as the Senior Team leader. If it's straight forward, I'll handle it; if the issue is large enough, I'll bring it to the rest of the Senior Team. If we had no Senior

Team, all these day to day problems would go to the pastoral staff, which is one of the reasons this structure works so well. It doesn't feel as 'heavy handed' for the prophetic people if it's me talking to them, instead of the pastor or elders. I can quite easily discuss issues or problems with the team members, because I have a rapport with them from working together in prophetic settings; they understand that we are all learning and that we learn by feedback.

If we didn't have a prophetic team, it would be far more difficult to deal with these day to day issues. Even little issues, left un-dealt with, lead to problems, which can lead to serious concerns; serious concerns not dealt with in a church generally leads to stifling of ministry in order to "deal with" the problem. (This applies in *any* ministry.) Furthermore, problems not dealt with in a timely, appropriate manner can lead to the demise of valuable, necessary functions in the church. In the team setting, we understand that we are all here with a common desire to develop ourselves and each other in the prophetic. We can accept instruction and correction regarding these day to day issues without someone getting offended.

The Senior Prophetic Team acts as a resource in the church for anyone wanting to submit prophetic words, be they dreams, warnings, visions or whatever. We encourage people to put forward any directional word to the Senior Prophetic Team. There's a lot of good testing that comes with this practice; the person submitting the word gets to be account-able. When people approach me with a revelation they have had, the first thing I ask them to do is to write it down so it can be evaluated. I would say that one in three ever actually get to the 'writing it down' stage.

Dreams are commonly what people want clarification on. I believe dreams are a valid way that God speaks to us, as we see throughout scripture. For example: Joseph and Mary being led by dreams out of

Jerusalem, then to Nazareth, for the protection of Jesus (Matthew 2: 19-23). Interpreting dreams isn't my strength, but the prophetic Senior Team is excellent at interpreting a dream using a group process. I have been amazed by how much information is gleaned as we work through the interpretation. It's like solving a puzzle, and there is a sense of accomplishment when the group together gets the answers to complete it.

Protection for the Pastor. The practice of submitting prophetic words for review is also a shield for the pastor, who is usually the one people have a word for. Often it's a directive word telling them what the pastor should be doing, or addressing some improvement they'd like to see. I feel quite strongly that these words should be evaluated by the Senior Team before the pastor or their spouse even hear or see them. Many times, the words are discouraging, and leave a dart of the enemy in their spirits. No one is more aware of their inadequacies than the pastors themselves, and even directional words have to be wrapped in comfort, edification and exhortation.

Protection for the Congregation. Submitting prophetic words for evaluation also protects the congregation from prophecy that may create fear, discord or uncertainty. One time I had a word submitted to me from a member of the Introductory Team. She and her husband had recently come from another church. They had talked to me about their interest in prophecy, but in a short conversation I could tell that the man had an Old Testament attitude towards the prophetic. I don't think he believed some of the teaching he'd received in the group about prophecy always being restorative, and he had challenged me on this. His wife surprised me when she emailed a prophecy on a Saturday afternoon wanting to give the word on Sunday morning. I hadn't ever really heard her prophesy, except indirectly in the Introductory Team activity, and she was very mild mannered, appearing more intercessory than prophetic. She emailed this prophecy telling of a natural disaster of significant proportion. Thankfully she had been in the church long enough to know she ought to submit it. Even if the word was 100% accurate, it would have been totally unacceptable to give that publically on a Sunday. She was virtually unknown, and had no track record prophetically within our church. She had never even prophesied in our church in the realm of comfort, edification or exhortation.

While we don't want to cast doubt on the validity of anyone's prophecy, any prophecy that is spectacular in nature, with potentially huge ramifications and/or potential to discredit the church should be carefully weighed (such as world events, nations, natural disasters). Additionally, the person delivering such a prophecy should have the trust and respect of those receiving the word, and furthermore, the setting/timing must be appropriate. Otherwise, it should be written down/recorded and kept until it is deemed appropriate; for instance, confirmed by another prophet who has a proven track record within the church.

I was able to email her back and tell her that while I appreciated her intercessory heart, Sunday morning would not be the appropriate time to give that word. Hopefully, she can respect this necessary step, and remain in a teachable attitude so that she may continue to develop in her gifting.

Provides Order. There is a continual stream of prophetic ministry as teams are called upon. All the requests are directed through me, as overseer. Even if a person goes to the pastor or the other elders with a request, they are told they have to talk to me. It's not that I'm a control freak; it just creates easier and clearer communication to establish an order of things. I can evaluate the request, see the time frame, and put it into context of whatever else is happening in the prophetic. That way, as overseer and co-ordinator, I also have a pulse on what ministry is going on in what area. Additionally, it stops people who have a tendency to go person to person asking for prophetic ministry. At one time when the church was smaller, all the leaders would have known what prophetic ministry was occurring in the church. Now that the church has grown, there are multiple ministries, and even the senior pastor doesn't know specifically what prophetic ministry is taking place unless he has recommended it. I just keep them apprised of any problems or issues that develop, and usually tell them how we solved it. It is important to keep communication flowing.

B. Benefits for the members

Builds Relationships. People with a strong prophetic gifting often feel misunderstood. I spent years of my life trying to mould myself into someone I just was not. When I started prophesying in the late seventies, there weren't any woman role models that I knew of, and I always felt as though I had to apologize for my gifting, wishing I could have something quiet and less public. Women seemed suspicious of me and men just plain weren't sure of how to work with a woman. But once we assembled a Senior Prophetic Team, even with our varied personalities in the group, I was comfortable, because we all had the love of the prophetic deep in our souls. Everyone longs for the camaraderie of others who are of like mind and really understand you. In prophetic ministry you go through a lot of experiences—sometimes crazy ones—that create a bond similar to a "you had to be there" feeling. We learned a lot from situations that went wrong, having to get through the best we were able, and a lot of our friendships developed through these times.

Accountability and Character Development. Accountability is necessary to keep a prophet from excess or just getting out of balance. We all seem to have some area where we must be diligent to guard against problems, whether it's melancholy, bitterness, cynicism, rationalization of sin or something else. As we meet, we are able to understand and discuss each other's challenges. We have used some material from

Bill Hammond[8] (a well-known, long-standing and experienced prophet) on character development. Examining our character is foundational to growth, and in my estimation, one of the most essential elements in facilitating development as a prophet.

In fact, one of the reasons a Senior Team member once gave for leaving the church was that he thought I put too much focus on character and not enough on gifting. That was fifteen years ago, and I feel stronger about it today than I did then. I'm sad to say that I've seen many instances where the most gifted person doesn't go the distance, and it comes down to character inadequacy. We have an enemy of our souls who is seeking whom he may devour—those with weak character, or those who resist character development may be an easy target.

Provides Opportunity for Personal Growth and Development. Ideas are bounced around, strategic planning is done for prophetic goals, upcoming ministry opportunities are discussed, as well as problem areas or people. These all contribute towards the development of leadership skills.

About the Members

The Senior Team has diversity in gifting and personality that indicates God assembled it. I would recommend considering diversity of members when you put together a Senior Team. Everything has not always gone perfectly, and there have been some ups and downs along the way. That is certainly part of the growing process.

Most of the individuals are also involved in other areas of ministry. Likely any one of us left on our own would be out of balance in one area of our lives or another, but together I think we bring out each other's best, and have a more balanced approach to governing the prophetic in the local church.

Members in Action

One time we were ministering as a prophetic team in a small town in Saskatchewan where my husband's brother and his wife pastor a church. One of the Senior Team members prophesied that a pastor would come to my brother-in-law and offer him his church and that where there were two churches, God would merge them together. About two years later, a pastor from the city approached my brother-in-law and told him that he'd never felt called to be the senior pastor, offered him his church, and said that he would also stay and be his associate. The senior pastor also had a church building, which was desperately needed by Scott's growing congregation. The churches successfully merged with the two pastors working together until 2011, when the former senior pastor retired peacefully. I'm not sure I've ever heard of another situation where a denominational church and a charismatic independent church came together to form a single congregation.

Levels of Functioning of Those at the Prophet Level

Throughout the book, I have been emphasizing development of the team ministry in the realm of comfort, edification and exhortation because I'm convinced that this is the way to promote widespread effective prophetic ministry within the church. However, there are those who are moving into a deeper level of the prophetic and could be referred to as "prophets". Once such people have proven track records in their ministry, including accuracy and a surrendered heart, they are free to step out into the deeper waters of revelation—guidance and direction, releasing strategies, foretelling, words of knowledge and wisdom. Once a prophet moves into this area, greater accountability is required, and there are more personal battles. While this is true, we still don't want people to shy away from the deeper levels of prophecy, especially once the individual is solid, and well trained in the prophetic. Once people prophesy on this deeper level, they continue to do so, but the prophecy is moderated while doing the "ministry between-services," because within that ministry, we ask the

Intermediate people to stay in the realm of comfort, edification and exhortation. The Senior person/prophet is a mentor, so the prophetic has to be limited in depth when ministering with that team.

When the prophet gets the opportunity to minister with other prophets, we see the level of prophetic anointing increase; however because our church has such a mandate for training, most often our prophets (Senior Team) are working with Intermediate group people in training and mentoring.

The resource pool for strategic direction, especially to the church leadership, is the Senior Team.

CHAPTER 7

HOW I WORK WITH SENIOR TEAM MEMBERS

Who is the leader?

The pastor may have to identify the prophetic leader, as many times the one meant to lead doesn't realize the depth of their call. Often, the pastor is the one to initiate prophetic ministry. Using myself as an example, there has never been any real question as to why I would be the leader of the Senior Team. Our pastor turned the ministry over to me shortly after we started prophetic teams, saying he really didn't have time, and that I clearly had the passion and vision for it (which I did). He saw a lot more in me than I saw in myself, as I didn't realize at the time the breadth of the ministry God was calling me to. This may be the case with a potential leader in your church. Before the Senior Prophetic Team even started, I was the "go to" person—and still am. The one to lead your prophetic team may be naturally acting in that capacity, but be unaware of their gifting to lead.

Accepting the challenge

Once the senior prophetic team was formed, I became aware that I had a responsibility to help us all develop both our character and gifting on a deeper level. By then it had been prophesied that "many prophets would be raised up out of Harvest City Church," and additionally, the training mandate over my life had been prophesied several times, as an encouraging confirmation.

Building the team

The Senior Team began meeting rather informally, discussing the prophetic overview of the church. We didn't have a strong agenda, but instead I used this time to find out how each one of us (and our families) was doing spiritually, emotionally, prophetically etc. This personal interaction would lead to people sharing their struggles with hearing from God, and making sense of what they were hearing. Ideas were pooled, and brainstorming sessions occurred at the meetings. People sometimes have the impression that prophets live on a consistently high spiritual plane. That's not usually the case; it's just that prophets can still prophesy even when they are hurting or having doubts, because the gifting doesn't simply stop. We want people to know that we value their whole person, not just their gifting, and the Senior meetings are a great place to work on that. We are also able to share a few laughs, because we all go through similar highs and lows. In a way, the Senior Team meetings are like a support group because they are small, intimate, and there is an atmosphere of trust. Even if there is no real agenda for a meeting, I will still try to meet every two months just so that we have a chance to update and relate.

I BELIEVE THAT I HAVE EXPERIENCED SUCCESS AS A LEADER BECAUSE THE TEAM MEMBERS KNOW THAT I WANT THEM TO SUCCEED.

I believe that I have experienced success as a leader because the team members know that I want them to succeed. They know I'm looking for opportunities for them where they can be stretched and expand their own gifting. They also know I stick up for them, doing my best to speak well of them to others. They know that even though we don't always agree or see things the same way, I value their input and appreciate their friendship. I believe that all of these things are important and valuable in the formation of a true team. The only time I have felt lack of support in the group was with one former member—he had his own ambitions and, I think, saw me as a barrier to his advancement. This can happen to any leader from time to time, and may even happen to you. To recognize that possibility and pray for God's guidance in advance will prepare you. I believe that you need to own your leadership without being a tyrant.

Real meaning of team practiced

The reason the team has stayed supportive and protective of me is that they know this isn't a competition. I have avoided one-upmanship and been really careful to work at building a team attitude, endeavouring to promote teamwork through my actions. I try to give everyone opportunity to participate in ministry. Even with our Senior Team in place, there is so much demand that it stretches us all. The restrictions of people's schedules and other ministry demands force us to work with whoever is available from the Senior Team. We are increasingly drawing in others to help from the Intermediate Team. I don't believe there is jealousy or competitiveness amongst the team members. There is more than enough ministry, and we have built our teams with an emphasis on servant-hood, not "prima donna" type ministry.

Generally, ministry times are inconvenient—you have to show up at times you'd rather stay at home, you get held up at meetings and services when you'd like to be out the door, and the planning, coordination and communication all take time. Everybody gets tested on their willingness to serve in the inconvenient times. We don't just camp on the prophetic peoples' gifting, we want them to get in there and serve. All of us must remember that respect is earned. I am protective to see the prophetic has a good reputation—I want the team members to act in such a way that people want them back, not just because of their ministry, but also because of their positive, serving attitudes.

We discuss what we are currently doing to develop our Introductory and Intermediate teams, overview the prophetic in the church, discuss areas of weakness and ideas for improvement. For a couple of years we worked through a character study called *The Making of a Prophet—Jim Wies*[9]. I think we all received personal benefit from that. We are concerned with developing our prophetic gifting, and God is concerned about developing our character.)

Don't delegate too quickly or too much

There is a lot of pressure to "mentor" and to delegate so that you can "replace yourself"—and there is wisdom in both. *Give people responsibilities they can handle.*

> WE ARE CONCERNED WITH DEVELOPING OUR PROPHETIC GIFTING, AND GOD IS CONCERNED ABOUT DEVELOPING OUR CHARACTER.

I deliberately give the team opportunities to grow, even though I know it will be uncomfortable and stretching for them.

I take team members whose strength is personal prophecy on ministry trips with me. That is a stretching experience, especially when approaching situations where you likely know nothing about the people you're ministering to. When ministering internally within your own church, chances are that you may know something about the person you are prophesying over.

There is always the temptation to use your best people for every ministry setting, but we want to develop all of our people, so I try to work with everyone in their areas of strength, but then push them beyond those areas. If someone likes to teach, I will give them the responsibility for teaching our prophetic team classes. For instance, I have on occasion delegated all the Introductory and Intermediate group teaching for an entire year. While that has been successful for the team members' personal growth, there are some reasons I won't do that regularly or for a prolonged period:

1. The introductory team people need to know my heart and vision for the prophetic.

2. It is a good idea to mix up the teaching and teachers so that new introductory people get to know the other Senior Team members. If the Senior Team members are familiar, they feel comfortable going to them with their questions, requests to be mentored, dreams to be interpreted, etc. That takes a big load off my shoulders.

3. When using various teachers, there is far less risk that someone will go 'off' in their teaching, or let some of their character weaknesses potentially harm the group.

   One of our Senior Team members was going in a different direction for at least a year before he left the church. While still in the church, he also had some unresolved resentments, and I feel that this came across in his teaching to the Introductory group. That would not have happened to the degree it did, had we been rotating the teaching schedule amongst the Senior Team. It's a whole lot easier to find people to teach just one class anyway, especially if I make myself available as a reference. I give them suggestions or assign a topic, and let them go ahead.

I also try to stretch the Senior people in personal prophecy by assigning them to minister with a person who is weaker in prophecy; this forces the Senior person to take the lead and prophesy first. I also look for "good fit" ministry opportunities outside the church, and include them in those opportunities.

For instance, if I know there are going to be a lot of young people where I am going to minister, I'll try to include the youngest on our team. There are countless benefits of having young adults minister—people are encouraged when they see young people prophesying with accuracy and anointing. Many times young people have never experienced other young people moving powerfully in their gifting, and it opens a whole world of possibilities to them. Ultimately it gives young people vision for their own life. Older people love being ministered to by young adults, as it confirms that God is really speaking when they hear such wise words through young voices. Repeatedly we get feedback that people are amazed how young people can prophesy—it is a testimony to God raising up the next generation.

In an effort to keep life and vision flowing, I also like to invite visiting ministers to spend time with the Senior Team and if possible, their spouses. I do this with incoming prophetic ministers but also with other speakers, as many of them are prophetic in combination with a teaching or preaching gift. These meetings are an opportunity for prophetic people to see the diversity in flavour and personality of prophets, as well as an opportunity to discover how things are done in other churches with regard to the prophetic. While we seldom come across a church with an actual prophetic team, many churches do have at least some protocol for the prophetic to move.

CHAPTER 8

HOW I WORK WITH PASTORS & ELDERS

Having a prophetic coordinator saves the pastors and elders time:

I am the 'go to' person for communication between the elders/pastor and the prophetic teams or individuals. I take the responsibility to investigate any issues that arise, and work closely with the church leadership and with the prophetic teams to find solutions. If for example, a prophetic person is out of line, the pastors will come to me to deal with it. Concerns that have arisen include inappropriate or incorrect public prophecy, and complaints about a prophecy given to an individual or within a home church setting. I have a strong working and personal relationship with most of the prophetic people, so it's easier for me, as opposed to an elder or the pastor, to address what can sometimes be challenging situations.

On the other hand, if the church leadership has done or recommended something that hasn't worked out, I have the liberty to discuss the issue with them and develop an appropriate resolution.

One of our elders had recommended that a young woman attend the Introductory Team meetings—he saw it as a way she could feel connected to the body of Christ. After a brief conversation with this woman, I realized she had a lot of needs, including what appeared to be mental health issues. I contacted the elder and explained that the woman was not a good candidate for prophetic team meetings. I felt she needed to come to terms with her issues before she began prophesying. The elder is a merciful counsellor; he understood, contacted the young woman, and was able to counsel her—steering her towards a home group. There she could build some relationships with people and meet her need for belonging.

A key to the success of the prophetic teams is that we are in submission to the elders, but also have the support and encouragement of the eldership.

Responsibilities of the prophetic coordinator:

- ➤ Make arrangements to bring in prophets to minister/teach in the church.
- ➤ Make arrangements for visiting pastors or missionaries to receive prophetic ministry.
- ➤ Review problems with any prophetic ministry in the church, in consultation with the elders and pastors, and take whatever action is needed.
- ➤ Provide informal reports to church elders and pastors about the prophetic teams, their activities, strategy and new members.
- ➤ Receive referrals from church leadership for new church members who may benefit from prophetic training or mentoring.
- ➤ Take agenda items to the eldership meeting from the prophetic team. (I make a request to be included on the agenda of the eldership meeting.) Usually I attend alone as a representative of the Senior Team. Other decisions discussed with the elders include: guidelines for house church prophetic ministry, guidelines for grade twelve graduate prophetic ministry, process for ministering to those being baptized, and organized ministry outside of the church. It is important to discuss these types of issues in order for the church to work together for the good of all.
- ➤ Create opportunities where the Senior Team members can build relationship with the elders. This can be done in different ways.

Examples: If a visiting speaker was known to have a prophetic gift, I'd try to arrange a social setting where the Senior Team can ask questions, and allow for general relationship building. The elders would be invited to an informal social setting, which helps the elders and the prophetic team get to know one other better. A few years ago I realized that while I had a lot of opportunity to get to know the church leaders, since I was part of the leadership team with my husband, the Senior Team did not. We found that these teaching and fellowship times help expand vision beyond the local church and help get a sense of what God is doing globally.

➢ Deliver and/or arrange a time for feedback from the elders to the prophetic teams. If the pastor wants to exhort the team in any area, he contacts me; we discuss the idea and the appropriate implementation.

Example: Once our pastor *really* exhorted the prophetic team with a specific suggestion: "We need more prophecy at baptisms. Come on you guys—stir yourselves up!" This incited a positive response, because it was such an affirmation of the support and backing of the senior pastor and elders.

Example: when we wanted to have a "Know Your Destiny" prophetic booth at the fairgrounds, our church leaders were not only supportive, they were downright excited about the possibly for evangelism, and making the church relevant to the community.

We get ongoing feedback from the pastors of how blessed they are as they hear testimonies about people who receive prophetic ministry from the teams. Church leaders are a major source of encouragement for us to develop and train others in the prophetic. By encouraging us, the church has a strong prophetic ministry to support future development and growth.

CHAPTER 9

GIVING FEEDBACK TO PROPHETIC PEOPLE

One of the duties—and privileges—of prophetic leaders and mentors is giving feedback and direction.

In my opinion, prophetic people generally fall into two categories: the first is those who need a lot of encouragement to step out in the gift they have; the second is those who have an elevated sense of their gifting and need to receive training in appropriate prophetic etiquette and gain a correct perspective of their gift. Both groups have their challenges, but the first group is more common and, in some ways, easier to deal with.

Group 1: The Under-Confident

These are people who would rather not put themselves forward, but when the Spirit of God comes on them they have a hard time *not* doing it. The anointing is what makes them want to go deeper and develop their prophetic gift. Prophetic team meetings are a place where they can feel accepted and learn from their mistakes. With encouragement, opportunity to prophesy, and positive feedback, they can readily develop the prophetic gifting God has ordained for them.

These people check with you or another authority when they "think" they might have a word that goes beyond comfort, edification or exhortation. They check if they feel they might have a word of knowledge. This approach builds trust between them and team leaders as well as church leadership. As they grow in confidence, these people can minister effectively in a team setting, with their words building on the words of others on the team.

They tend to stay connected with the prophetic team meetings because it gives them opportunity to prophesy and maintain confidence that they are hearing from God. Once they are comfortable ministering within the church, I like to encourage these people to use their gift in practical, everyday ways. They can stretch themselves in their day-to-day lives by reaching out to others God is speaking to them about. They can phone or contact the people God places on their heart to offer words of comfort, send cards of encouragement, or give words of knowledge as they are directed. These people respond to praise, flourish in the prophetic environment and will live a fulfilled life prophesying in the realm of comfort, edification or exhortation. And not only do they receive personal fulfillment, they are a blessing both to the body of Christ and beyond, making a difference in the world around them.

Group 2: The Over-Confident

These people usually have a powerful and obvious prophetic gifting. However, they can be more difficult to work with because they think they are at a higher level prophetically than they actually are. This typically leads them into problems when they use their gift, and can strain relations between them, other church members and leadership. Many such people come from other churches or ministry circles where they haven't had to be accountable. Sometimes they have had previous teaching or training, from Bible School for example, so they feel that they are ready for a public ministry.

Prophetic team meetings can help these people to get a better estimation of their gift. They may discover they aren't as accurate or prolific as they think. Involving these people in ministry to the uncharted also provides a healthy check on their gifting. Secular people are very direct in their feedback, and this group of people can really benefit from frank and independent feedback to their words. If they appreciate that they do have more to learn, and if I can gain their respect, then I can work with them. It helps when they can see that our church leadership supports me and has given me authority.

Over the years I have met with various people who are trying to fast track their way to a strong prophetic voice or being a great prophet. When we first meet, I think they are surprised when I want to know: Do they have a job? A family? How are they handling the practical matters of life?

My husband and I once met with a man who didn't want to talk about anything in his life except the powerful dreams he had. He wanted us to provide one-on-one mentoring for him so that he could develop as a prophet as soon as possible. We talked to him about his character, about gaining solid employment, taking responsibility for his family and being faithful in the small things. I told him if he wanted to write down his prophetic dreams and visions I would present them to the Senior Team for evaluation. A year passed since that meeting and I have yet to receive anything. I've given him an opportunity to demon-strate character so that I can work with him. Right now he really hasn't earned the right to be mentored as a prophet until he gets some things sorted out in his personal life. My responsibility is to God and the church leadership, so I can't promote someone who doesn't show the character that ought to go along with their gifting. This man's sense of entitlement is getting in the way of his growth and development in the prophetic. I suspect he may grow impatient with our emphasis on character and find another church.

Sometimes I meet people with a genuine prophetic gifting but who require a lot of attention. A young woman came to our prophetic team meetings from another church. She was quick to let me know that she had been on that church's prophetic ministry team and was in fact one of the leaders. During the first team meeting she attended, it was evident that she was not as mature as she thought. To begin with, she shared too much personal and inappropriate information about herself, which made other team members quite uncomfortable. This is a loveable girl who has a good heart, but she has some challenges she will have to overcome in order to minister, including a health challenge, which seems to be the root of some of her difficulties. She often tries to dominate a sharing time and has to be reined in during prophetic ministry. For instance, while we were ministering to someone in a group setting, this woman was praying so loudly that she drowned out one of the elders while he was ministering to another person. I had to put my hand on her back and tell her to stop. She doesn't seem to be aware that she is too loud or that she often encroaches on other's personal space. She will come too close to a person when she is speaking, which puts them off. Even though this may be due to her disability, she has to manage her behaviour if she is to minister effectively. We don't get to choose those God blesses with a prophetic gift, and have to work with the personalities in which the gift is contained.

Even though I was prepared to work with this person, she has since withdrawn from all prophetic teaching and involvement. I think it became apparent that we are as or more concerned with character development as we are with releasing prophetic gifting. This wasn't a success story but it gives the picture of the variety of people you will work with as you develop prophetic teams.

Some Common Feedback Areas

Incomprehensible prophecies... Something I have had to give people feedback about over the years is elaborate prophecies that don't have a clear interpretation. We really emphasise that prophecy has to make sense to people. It's okay to share a picture or vision in a team ministry situation, since someone else on the team may have the interpretation.

But in a public meeting, each prophecy needs to make sense on its own, without further explanation.

Distracting manifestations... Sometimes when people are prophesying, the power of the Holy Spirit is so strong that they shake or they may groan or make other odd sounds. If this becomes a pattern, I take the person aside and gently advise them to wait and prophesy when they have a better grip on themselves. I know this is a sensitive area, and some may disagree with me, but my conviction is that distracting manifestations take away from a prophecy and the clarity of what is being said. 1 Corinthians 14:78 cautions us: "*If even inanimate musical instruments, such as the flute or the harp, do not give distinct notes, how will anyone (listening) know or understand what is played? And if the war bugle gives an uncertain (indistinct) call, who will prepare for battle?*"

Extraneous details... Sometimes the person prophesying can include information that is not necessary and actually hinders others from receiving the word.

Example: A middle aged man prophesied quite regularly in our Sunday meetings. He was somewhat overweight, and started several of his prophecies by saying, "When I was in the shower this morning God spoke to me..." The congregation couldn't get past the picture of this man in the shower, and were not able to focus on what he was saying prophetically. Even though giving feedback in this kind of situation can be awkward, that man had to be told to leave out the particulars of where he received the word.

Modeling prophecy... Prophecy is not just about the word given and its accuracy, it's also about the person giving the word, and who they are as an individual. If your heart and motives are not to bless the body of Christ, people aren't interested in what you have to say—no matter how perfect the word is. You have to earn people's respect if you are to be heard.

Example: At a worship meeting, one of our team members prophesied about "going the distance for God," and challenged the congregation to do just that. Then right after she gave the word she left the meeting! From the perspective of the Church, it appeared her actions didn't live up to the exhortation, and that hurt her credibility.

Timing... Learning to give a word at the right time is really tricky and takes time to develop. During worship is often an opportune time. In our church, people who want to prophesy are required to go to first and ask the pastor or meeting leader, and use the microphone, which is usually held by the pastor or person coordinating the meeting. If the prophecy is being presented during worship, wait for the song to end or for a signal from the worship leader. Worship leaders who have been in the prophetic environment long enough know to keep an eye out for someone coming forward to give a prophetic word.

It is usually best to give a word that is in the same flow as the meeting. If it's an upbeat praise time, the word should go along with that; if it's a more reverent moment, the prophetic word should follow that flow. Put yourself in the worship leaders' shoes: it's really difficult for them to have brought people into "the high praises of God" and then have someone give a sobering prophetic word. The unfortunate worship leader now has to pick up the congregation and get them back to the same level as before the word. It's not that worship leaders won't be gracious, as this does happen from time to time, but it's best to avoid it wherever possible.

Sometimes, if the worship is winding down and the meeting coordinator is eager to get on to the next part of the service, he will ask the person to wait to give the word another time. This does not mean there was anything wrong with the word; it's just not the right time for it.

Once people are more experienced in the prophetic, it is easier to get the timing right. Even so, I still have times where I'm not sure whether a word is a "now" word or one that needs to be kept for another occasion. Does God want it to marinate, to add more to it? I recall one time when I received a word that I decided not to share the first time it came to me. I went to three services in a row, but it never seemed to be the right occasion for that word. Still, it was growing inside of me and I felt an urgency to share it. Finally I got a message in my spirit that I needed to share the word with the whole congregation on a specific Sunday, in both our early and late services. I approached our pastor and his wife about it and they both felt that the word was intended to be given on that Sunday was the confirmation I needed.

Many times people are fearful that if they miss an opportunity to give a word they have really failed the Lord. I encourage people to hang on to the word and seek God for another opportunity. If there doesn't seem to be one, they can write the word down and submit it to the Senior Prophetic Team, especially if it is a word that went along with the theme of the meeting. It can still be word of blessing, even if it isn't given publicly.

MANY TIMES PEOPLE ARE FEARFUL THAT IF THEY MISS AN OPPORTUNITY TO GIVE A WORD THEY HAVE REALLY FAILED THE LORD.

Give only what you have received... Sometimes people give a prophecy that starts out fine. The hearers are receiving the word and sense the heartbeat of God. But sometimes the person prophesying doesn't know how or when to stop and the word goes flat. When that happens, I try to speak to the prophetic person and, using that exact prophecy as the example, suggest where they could have ended the prophecy. That way they can have more confidence the next time to give just what they have received.

Keep it focused... When prophecy is too lengthy, people in the congregation just stop listening. If a person repeatedly prophesies in that manner, the congregation loses respect for them and rarely benefits from relevant portions of the word.

One girl who was experienced in prophecy but had more of an intercessory style got up to prophesy, and carried on...for ten minutes. It was terrible! Everyone was cringing as the word went on and on. Also, as she prophesied she referred to God as "Daddy." In most people's minds there is something not quite right when forty and fifty-somethings call God "Daddy." I tried to work with that woman to help her, but I think she felt that she was more spiritual than I.

Stay on one theme... I have heard people who have a strong prophetic word lose the impact in delivery when they are including too many themes in one prophecy. Keep the main thing the main thing. We need to help one another keep in mind that going in multiple directions during the same prophecy is confusing to those who are listening. For example: If you have a prophecy about the blood of Jesus, don't include Adam and Eve in the garden and a random quote from a major prophet. Stick with the blood, and let the Holy Spirit give you words that flow and build on that theme alone.

Feedback Guidelines

I use the following guidelines when providing feedback to prophetic people:

1. Look for a specific pattern in behaviour or style, so the person doesn't feel like one particular occurrence is being pounced on.

2. Identify a concrete example to speak to. I find if you talk to people in general terms, they don't understand what you are

trying to say, but if you can directly discuss an incident or occasion, it is easier for them to understand.

3. Don't take an authoritative or a top-down approach. Try to come alongside the person, being like Barnabas, "the son of encouragement." Don't lord your authority over them, but speak to them as a friend. I take the approach that it's just like Aquila and Priscilla instructed Apollos "more perfectly" or accurately (Acts 18: 24-26). When we come alongside to encourage someone, it is like a friend, not an authority figure.

4. Use a '**sandwich approach**': begin with a positive statement, then the correction, and then end with encouragement. Be clear that change needs to occur, but never humiliate or embarrass. I remind myself that this is an opportunity to connect with the person, find out what is going on in their life and build relationship with them. Be sure to leave things on a positive note so that the person doesn't beat themselves up. I know that kind of condemnation is a devilish tactic, and can cause a person to become depressed or give up on their gift altogether, so it's very important to encompass correction with encouragement.

5. Share about a time when you have failed, so they know that we all go through the growth and development process. Unfortunately, I have many such stories to share.

6. If people have a blind spot, they must be told. When a person is part of a team they can receive feedback because they know that's what the team is for—to watch each other's back and help one another develop their gifting.

7. Let the prophetic people know you are on their side. I understand how hard it is to "get it right" in the prophetic. Learning

to give the right word, at the right time and in the right place takes maturity—and that is usually learned by trial and error.

8. After meeting with someone to address an issue, find an occasion to show that you trust them. The sooner the better. For example, I may invite them to participate in an opportunity to prophesy, or invite them to share something with the prophetic team at a meeting. I just look for some way to express my faith in them and their gifting, and encourage them to move forward.

9. When dealing with an individual of the opposite sex, ask someone of the same sex on the Senior Team to meet with them for follow-up (i.e: man to man, woman to woman). As a woman, I try not to have ongoing meetings with one man unless one of the other Senior Team members is with me. Even though it's common for me to work with men, I find it's wise to be careful in such situations.

Final Thoughts on Feedback

One of my biggest goals is to give a continual flow of positive encouragement to both individuals and teams. I go to the Romans 2:4 principle: that it is the kindness of God that draws us to repentance (or change). I think too many prophetic people are already abundantly aware of their failures and inadequacies. Our adversary, the devil, wants people locked into a negative mindset. He wants people so discouraged with themselves that they don't have the faith to prophesy. He is afraid of the results, of how much good can be done in and through the body of Christ when empowered believers speak out on God's behalf.

Prophetic people face formidable battles, so we need to develop habits of right thinking. We speak often in our team meetings of taking authority over our minds. I think we need to exercise our minds every day to stay positive. Alcoholics Anonymous encourages its people to stay away from "stinking thinking." Philippians 4:8 says, "Finally, brothers and sisters, whatever is true, whatever is noble, whatever is right, whatever is pure, whatever is lovely, whatever is admirable—if anything is excellent or praiseworthy—think about such things" (NIV). I don't think we can accurately and effectively reflect the heart of God unless we continually strive to have our minds renewed, but as we do that, we become vessels that pour out sweet anointing for Him.

CHAPTER 10

DEALING WITH PROBLEMS

The prophetic, like any other ministry, can easily be misunderstood. You will inevitably have to deal with problems. Following are some lessons that I have learned through practical experience in a variety of situations:

"Negative" Prophecy

Although I believe prophecy should always be in the realm of encouragement, comfort and edification, there are times when a particular word can be uncomfortable for a person to receive. In such instances the "prophet" has to use wisdom.

One time we were ministering to a couple in a home group. They were expecting their first child. The person prophesying had a son born with a heart condition, which required several surgeries over the years. He began to prophesy over this couple that they would be just like him and his wife. He said, "I feel like God may give you a challenging child, but you have to understand that it will be used for His good—for His glory." He prophesied that it was going to be a significant challenge, but God would give them the grace to deal with it, and through this situation they would have many open doors to minister to others. The couple was distressed, the home group leaders were distressed, and the elders who heard about it after weren't especially happy, as the couple needed pastoral care to help them cope with this word.

As it turned out, their baby was born perfectly healthy. Two years later, they had a second child....born with Down Syndrome. The parents were completely shocked, as this had not been diagnosed during the pregnancy. Just as the word was prophesied, the couple has had tremendous grace in dealing with and living with the challenge of having a child with a disability; in fact, they named her Grace. The couple are still in church, serving and growing in God, and even have a desire to adopt another child with Down Syndrome. The revelation had been accurate, but it would have been better to have spoken to the home group leaders, and let them decide how, or if, that word should be submitted to the couple.

Public Prophecy

There are those who give repetitive or vague prophecy in very public settings. When that happens—especially from the same people—the congregation starts to ignore others who do come with clear and accurate words. It has a profoundly negative impact on the service as well. When prophecy is not uplifting or strong, the worship team or meeting leader has to work harder to restore the flow of the meeting, and help bring the congregation back into the presence of the Lord.

Week after week, two members of the prophetic team would prophesy in our Sunday services. The prophecies were somewhat repetitive and vague, but not harmful. The church leadership asked me to speak to them. First, I let them know that I really had appreciated their efforts to step out and prophesy, and then pointed out that a lot of their words had been quite similar. I asked them to take a break for a time and allow opportunity for others to prophesy.

Abuse of Prophecy

The time to have prophetic ministry is when you are building the church, the church is well established, or new territory is being launched. Prophetic ministry can help identify leaders, gifts and callings of the church and impart ongoing vision.

I've heard that some churches call in prophetic ministry when things are about to implode, hoping that prophetic ministry will set everyone straight. I was once invited to prophesy at a church where the leaders and pastor were in conflict. I held prophetic sessions over the weekend and had a message prepared for the Sunday service. However, Saturday night the Lord started speaking to me about Ezra and rebuilding the walls, with a specific application to the fractured situation in the church. I knew God was speaking to me prophetically, but I wasn't used to launching off from a prophetic word when speaking to a congregation. I called my own pastor and asked him what he thought I should do. He encouraged me and gave me the confidence to go with the prophetic word.

As it turned out, what I spoke was exactly what they needed to hear. I left that situation content that I had been obedient. Unfortunately, that congregation didn't stay together, but that was a consequence of their own decisions.

Managing Prophetic People

We have approximately fifty people in our Intermediate Prophetic Team. They are all able to minister in public, but it's not always easy finding enough opportunities. Prophetic people need to prophesy, and when they cannot find an outlet they can become disgruntled. Some of the members of our Intermediate Team were upset that they were not being used, so I called the group together, assuring them that they would each get an opportunity to minister, but they had to be patient. I pointed out that some had been members of the team for only a year, while others had been serving faithfully for more than a decade. I also mentioned that we have a very large pool of "prophetic people."

We then did a ministry time where they first prophesied over each other, and then I had the Introductory group come in and receive ministry. One of the Introductory Team members had been faithfully attending all year, but I had noticed in the practical activity times that he was not getting a release to prophesy. That night a few of us prayed and prophesied over him, and took authority over the strongholds that were hindering him from the release of prophecy. That was a breakthrough night for him, and the team could see real results from their ministry. It helped everyone appreciate that prophecy can happen any time, any place and is not restricted to formal ministry sessions.

Principles for Problem Solving

1. Treat the problem as a learning experience for both the prophetic person and the receiver. Don't ignore small adjustments as people are learning. If the small opportunities are ignored, the person will plough on and eventually make a big mistake.

2. Address "the problem" with a mature attitude. In more than 90% of the ministry we do, we are blessed with positive results. Of course there will be adjustments required along the way, but we need to keep our focus positive, and not dwell on the odd mistake.

3. Get all of the facts, and don't over react. Solicit the opinions of those involved—giver and receiver. If you can, listen to the recording of the word and make your own assessment. Discuss and tactfully correct the situation with both the giver of the prophecy *and* the receiver.

   I had a situation where a prophetic person referred to marriage when prophesying over a dating couple. Even though it would have been better not to use the term marriage, I also didn't want to overreact to the situation. I spoke to the couple and the person who gave the prophecy and explained the person ministering to them saw them working together in ministry, and used the term "married," but that may not have been accurate.

I encouraged them to focus on the overall word given to them. The prophetic person understood they made a mistake, and it will serve to make them more careful in the future.

4. Always listen to the full prophecy, and focus on the overall message. Sometimes a person prophesies as though the word is yet to come, when in reality it may have already happened. Prophetically, the timing of events in a person's life is hard to discern, but it doesn't make the word less accurate. Encourage people to take the big picture viewpoint, and put what isn't clear on the shelf. Sometimes people discount the whole word, saying, "This event already happened to me," when they should be paying attention to the rest of the prophecy.

CHAPTER 11

CORE CONCEPTS FOR BUILDING PROPHETIC MINISTRY FOUNDATIONS

1. The kindness (love) of God draws us to repentance (Romans 2:4 NASB).

This is a foundational principle that needs to apply to absolutely everyone who prophesies. It is also how I pray and speak into people's lives. Even when God identifies sin and hard-heartedness in our lives, He desires to draw us to himself. When we prophesy over people, no matter what God shows us, it has to be presented in a redemptive manner. People have a tendency to run away from God when shown their true motives, just like Adam and Eve hid from God in the garden. Romans 8: 35-39 tells us that nothing can separate us from the love of God, and that includes prophecy. God may present people with choices or tell them the consequences of their decisions, but His heart is one of love for us all, therefore He always desires restoration, offering a path to more intimate relationship with Himself.

2. The motive for ministry is to serve and bless.

Fruitfulness in prophetic ministry, or any ministry for that matter, comes down to our motives. Are the deep motives of our hearts—not just in prophetic ministry but generally speaking—to see churches raised up and strengthened? Is our motive like Nehemiah's: to see walls rebuilt and new walls being constructed? If so, you can be sure God is with you, and function in confidence and authority. Any time I am battling fear or intimidation in ministry, the solution is to examine my motives.

But how do I know for sure what my motives are? As the prophet Jeremiah said, *"The heart is deceitful above all things, And desperately wicked; who can know it?"* (Jeremiah 17: 9 KJV). I have discovered a rule of thumb: when I am functioning out of a kingdom motive, I am prepared to make the necessary sacrifices.

Prophetic ministry is inconvenient; I may need to come early before a service, or stay late. I often minister when it's a bad time for me but convenient for the people receiving ministry. There have been many times I have had to travel and minister when I just did not feel like I was up to it. If I pass the test of ministering despite inconvenience, then I know I'm not doing it for my own gain.

Recently I was heading off to minister in a remote area, quite a distance away, requiring me to take four flights to get there. As it was nearing time for the trip, I began a grumbling conversation with God about how this was a lot of work and trouble for possibly not that many people. I rambled on about the time of year, being away from my family, the sacrifice I was making etc. I suddenly had a very clear response from the Holy Spirit saying, "Try dying for one." My heart was smitten immediately, as though pierced with an arrow, causing yet another attitude adjustment in my journey of many.

Some people just don't want to be inconvenienced. Others only want to be available for the high profile prophetic ministry. The measure I use to evaluate the dedication of prophetic team members is: how willing are they to put themselves out to minister sacrificially? This willingness or unwillingness on a member's part tells me all I need to know about how far they will go in the prophetic ministry.

"...whoever wants to become great among you must be your servant, and whoever wants to be first must be your slave—just as the Son of Man did

not come to be served, but to serve, and to give his life as a ransom for many" (Mathew 28: 26-28 NIV).

One of the biggest sacrifices is being willing to be misunderstood. Using myself as an example, my nature is to explain myself, to justify what I'm doing. I often have to take time off from my secular job, usually an extra day or two combined with a weekend, for ministry travel. Other times I'm off for several days. My boss and colleagues at work know I offer workshops and do something "spiritual," but I have become aware that some people think I'm just slacking off and taking a holiday. I have to continually commit this to the Lord and trust Him to hide me under the shadow of His wings. I have to be willing to be misunderstood and resist defending myself, knowing that if I stay faithful to what He has called me to do, He will look after the details and judgements of others. My motivation must remain "to serve and to bless," regardless of what others may think of me.

3. Character is key.

This principle would be the deal breaker of all principles when I consider those who have the greatest gifting, and what impedes them from following their full calling. There are strongly gifted prophetic people who have let their gift go by the wayside because they didn't want to do the character development that goes with the gift. I have been accused of being too focused on this area, but I just don't see people fully developing their prophetic gifting if they aren't willing to be faithful in the small things. I have had my disappointments with people in this area. I count on team members for scheduled ministry only to see some cancel at the last minute. I often ask less gifted people to minister, considering instead, their faithfulness, and knowing they can be counted upon.

God tests our character and commitment. I once had a visiting minister billeted in our home. We blessed him and made him comfortable. I cooked really nice meals for him. But I did not like him. He was arrogant and continually talked about how things in his church were better than ours.

On Sunday, as he was speaking and I was thinking, "Thank God, he'll be gone soon," God began to speak to me prophetically about this man. It was a good word of exhortation and direction about God taking him to another level spiritually. I resisted the prophecy. I asked God, "You know I don't like him—why should I prophesy over him? Why should I bless him? You can see how full of himself he is! What if my spirit of dislike comes through in the prophecy?"

Then I got it. Am I running the show or is God? Was I willing to be faithful to the gift God had given me, to use it how He wanted me to? Was I going to decide who I would and wouldn't prophesy over? I put myself in servant mode and gave the word. Who knows what God's priority was? Did He just want to test my will or did He just really want to bless this man? It was probably both, but I did learn something that day: to be a servant, you need to do the things you are called to do, regardless of your own feelings or desires.

4. Be a team player

In our church, we are all about team ministry—from the pastor and his wife on down. When someone is focused on building their own ministry, it stands out. It's interesting to note that when we go to other churches, they are impressed with the "flavour" of our church coming through in our prophetic ministry. I think it's because of the team attitude—an understanding that the Kingdom is not about building individual ministries. Even though I'm officially "head" of the prophetic ministry in our church, I refer to myself as the coordinator. We really don't encourage anyone to prophesy without having a leader present to judge the prophecy. If I unexpectedly have a word over someone, I try to call over another leader to stand with me during the prophecy. This just avoids any possible confusion or misunderstanding. It is so much easier, especially as you are learning and developing prophecy on a team.

Joel (Senior Team member, at the time) and I were prophesying one time over a young man. When we saw him a few days later and asked him how he felt about the word, he said it was okay, but that he didn't like the part where God wanted to discipline him. He said he wasn't so sure about that part of the prophecy. Joel and I were shocked because we hadn't said anything about God disciplining him. Then I remembered we had said that God wanted to build the "disciplines" in his life. Those would be things like regular prayer, Bible reading, Bible meditation and worship. The enemy had taken one word and really twisted it in this man's mind. Without two people having been present, one could easily question whether they had, in fact, said it correctly, causing doubt and confusion to both giver *and* receiver. In general, it is good practice not to prophesy alone. You have to be really accomplished or experienced in the prophetic to prophesy on your own.

5. Prophetic people need to prophesy.

I was invited to come to a church to conduct a workshop on prophecy. They had been studying the prophetic for a year, and had a 600 page manual they used for teaching. I honestly wondered why they would want me to come in for further teaching. At the beginning of the workshop I asked how many of them had prophesied before. Not a single person put up their hand. I couldn't believe it! All the study in the world can't develop prophetic gifting without practical application. We have to step out in faith and actually prophesy. People with a strong prophetic gifting get restless if there is no opportunity for them to prophesy. That restlessness leads to criticism of the church and then offense that their gift is not recognized. It's a toxic situation which puts prophetic people and church leadership at odds with each other. A prophetic team that is focused on serving the congregation under the authority of the church leadership creates a healthy balance. Prophetic people can have a bit of an edge to them, but if they are managed appropriately and given the opportunity to contribute to the life of a church, they can become a tremendous blessing. If you are prophesying, you should be a part of the team. When you are part of the team you become accountable for your actions, with opportunity to learn from your mistakes.

6. Include the Group in Decision-Making

I take decisions to the prophetic team or to the elders so we can all be in agreement about how we will handle specific kinds of situations. If I don't agree with the others' decision, I will do my best to help them see my point of view, but ultimately I will follow the wishes of the group at large. Sometimes I'm quite sure the group's decision won't work, but I have to let it play out, and then make whatever changes are necessary later.

I once heard an illustration about a girl riding on the back of her dad's hay wagon. She was standing up straight and getting tossed off balance with every bump in the road. Her dad yelled back to her, "It's a lot easier if you bend your knees!" I often think of that story as an analogy when a decision needs to be made or a process changed—it's easier if you yield, or "bend your knees," so that you glide over the bumps instead of getting stalled by them.

7. Be Consistent

What you do for one, you must be prepared to do for all. Making these decisions as a group will (as above), help provide for consistency.

Here are some examples of decision-making issues (which also caused me to practice "bending my knees"):

- Should we include children in the between-service Sunday prophetic ministry times? If so, what guidelines will we follow? (Parental permission, parents present.)

- Can people from outside the church receive prophetic ministry at a home group that is part of our church?
- Do we minister to all grade twelve students in the church? Should it be limited to the Christian school only?
- Do we provide prophetic ministry for anyone who requests it? What are our guidelines?
- Should some people be able to skip the introductory prophetic meetings and fast track to minister with an intermediate team?
- Do we provide ministry for all small groups, or should they be encouraged to attend the 'between-service ministry' already available?
- Should we schedule prophetic ministry for children's church? If so should this be an annual event?
- How should we approach mentoring individuals in the prophetic?
- Should both the first and second year Bible School students receive prophetic ministry?
- How do we make the congregation aware of the prophetic?
- Should we participate in the newcomers' classes?
- How do we handle the ministry around water baptisms?
- What are the ministry guidelines for our missionary partners?

We have such a broad variety of stakeholders and situations that it's vital for us to be consistent. Even if you have a very small group or limited prophetic responsibilities at this time, it is still extremely important to be consistent. Always try to be fair and at the same time realize that processes have to change and adapt as we grow and move forward.

8. Keep the prophetic relevant and continually evaluate.

How relevant is prophecy to the majority of people in the congregation? Making prophetic ministry available between services was a huge step we took in trying to make prophetic ministry meaningful to the larger congregation. Prophesying over people at water baptisms is another. Ministry to grade twelve students in the Christian school is also an example.

If new people or the congregation at large can't relate to prophecy, work at ways to increase your relevance and effectiveness.

CHAPTER 12

PRAYER–THE FOUNDATION FOR PROPHETIC MINISTRY

Ministering effectively in the prophetic requires an anointing to prophesy. God is the one Who anoints. In order to prophesy "on demand," God and His Word must be the foundation of your life, and your relationship with Him must be constant. Discipline is a factor in doing anything well, and discipline requires consistency. I learned very early on in my Christian walk, even before I had a prophetic ministry, that I couldn't live without prayer and Bible reading start to my day— every day. Because my personality was strong, I not only had the quick Irish wit, but also the quick Irish sharp tongue. I was afraid to go out of the house without prayer and Bible reading as a covering for me, because of how I might act and what I might say. As I look back, recognizing this weakness in myself early and placing my dependency on God to keep me walking straight has enabled me to lay the proper foundations in my life. Regular prayer and Bible reading are just so that I can function as a Christian; this is not enough for prophetic ministry.

When there is planned prophetic ministry, I have to set aside time to pray and hear what God is wanting to speak to me. Prayer and worship go hand in hand. Before a scheduled prophetic ministry, I like to have the names of those that will be ministered to. I likely don't know them, but I need to pray for them anyway. Sometimes God will speak to me about the person or situation in these dedicated prayer times, but most often, He doesn't. I often don't get the prophetic information until I am actually in the location where the ministry is to occur. Some of the preparation process usually includes some fasting. I'm not doing God any favours through the fast—it's for me to shake off dullness and be able to hear more clearly. I find fasting helps my focus; it helps me get a Godly perspective, instead of a fleshly one. For me personally, I have to be very guarded about what I'm viewing and reading during this time, including the time leading up to the ministry. Many things are not wrong or immoral, but they are distractions. Prophetic ministry requires focus.

There is an aspect to the preparation and carrying out the prophetic ministry that is "... *(laying) hold of that for which Jesus Christ has also laid hold of me*" (Phillipians 3:12 NKJV). Through prayer, we grab onto and claim what the Father has already intended for those people. Prayer brings about the full purpose of God. Prayer is the springboard for prophecy. In training people to use their prophetic gifting, I suggest they prepare themselves, but I give nothing specific. I mention fasting but leave it up to the individual to do what they feel God is telling them to do.

Preparation for ministry through prayer gives me confidence, and helps me feel ready to conquer what God has shown me. However it is not a formula. I never think or teach that it is proportionate. For example, thinking that one hour of prayer should be good for one hour of ministry is not correct thinking. Once you are functioning in regular prophetic ministry, or are a prophet, you can be called upon with no notice to give prophetic input into people's lives and situations, and you can prophesy with *seemingly* no preparatory prayer. The preparation happens on a daily basis—with a foundation of prayer. You minister out of a well—out of a reserve that is built up by coming regularly into God's presence. In this way, you are not a foreigner to hearing what God has to say in the unexpected moments.

CHAPTER 13

PROPHETIC VISION & DESTINY

Many people think prophecy is a way to find the will of God for their lives. If they could 'just get a word,' a tough decision would become so much easier. Should I take this job? Marry this person? Go on that mission trip? In fact, prophecy is very much linked to discovering God's will for your life, but the way it operates is quite different than many imagine.

There are certainly times that God will speak prophetically into the details of daily life, but most often God speaks to the big picture—your destiny. Once a person understands their destiny, which I would define as: "God's vision and purpose for their life," it becomes much easier to make the day to day decisions.

One of my greatest desires is to see the entire body of Christ released in the destiny that God has purposed for individual lives. What a tragedy it is when people simply pass through life, never taking the time to discover the dream God has put inside them, allowing themselves to reach the end of their life with regrets that they didn't even make an attempt to see their most precious God-inspired desires come to pass; never

PROPHECY CAN HELP US BREAK OUT OF OUR COMFORT ZONE, OVER-COME OUR FEARS...AND REALIZE OUR DESTINY.

taking the risk to step out in faith and pursue their God-given destiny. Prophecy can help us break out of our comfort zone, overcome our fears, and provide the necessary focus and drive to overcome obstacles and realize our destiny.

A twelfth grade student in our Christian school competes in track and field at a national level. Her coach thinks she has the ability to compete and win international competitions, possibly even the Olympics. While still in the eighth grade, this girl received a prophecy that talked about her greatness in track and field—declaring that she would be like a Catriona Le May Doan (Canadian Olympic speed skater). That word was given before she even started training in track; now it is really exciting to see this girl live out her God-given dreams. She has tremendous focus and the drive to realize her destiny in athletics. No sloppy living for her, and prophecy is partly responsible for that!

A long-time friend and church member had an opportunity to attend a national prayer assembly in response to the Prime Minister's apology to First Nations and Aboriginal people for the abuse they suffered in residential schools. She is a public school teacher, and had to take two days off work to attend. When she talked to her principal about it, he asked if she would be willing to share about the event with the staff when she got back, and he gave her time off with pay to attend. She remembered a prophetic word that had been given to her a year before. It was said that she would have favour in her workplace to take mission-like opportunities. Normally a timid person, that prophetic word helped her to realize this was God's plan for her, and she was able to participate with greater boldness and confidence.

When God speaks destiny into your life through a prophetic word it typically starts a journey that can be long, distressing, and usually leads to significant change in your life. You have to approach destiny like a pilgrimage in which you cannot see the end of the path you are to walk. There will be many twists and turns along the way, perhaps even some setbacks, but you'll get there if you persevere—keeping your eyes on

Jesus, *"the author and perfecter of our faith"* (Hebrews 12: 2 NAS). The prophetic gives you something concrete to hold on to and helps you to remain faithful.

In the summer of 2009 I was in a real slump. God had been speaking to my husband and me about transition and change. We decided to downsize from a family home and buy a condo to free up more time to serve God. We believed that God had given us the green light to purchase the condo so we went ahead; the only problem was our house just would not sell. For six months we paid the mortgage on both properties which put a real strain on our financial resources. We had two offers on our house, but both fell through at the last minute. The second deal fell through the day before we were leaving for holiday on Vancouver Island. I was so filled with despair that I could not relax and enjoy the vacation. At night I'd lay awake and analyze what went wrong with each offer. I'd examine every area of our lives to determine if we were out of God's will.

We were staying with my sister and her husband, who are not believers, so I was trying harder than ever to convince her that a life with God is the greatest, while inside I was having serious doubts. I knew I was avoiding looking up old friends because I didn't want to be around believers who had "everything going great" in their lives while I was feeling like a loser. I couldn't determine the source of the problems, and besides, God was my best friend, so this was even more confusing. My husband, Todd, was completely unfazed. He was relaxed and seemed to have no concerns about our situation.

One afternoon we went to tour a famous army fort on Vancouver Island. When we got there I thought, "Who am I kidding?" I couldn't care less about seeing an army fort. I knew Todd would want to read every plaque and not miss a single detail, and I knew I'd be going crazy with impatience. When we got there I said, "Why don't you go ahead?

I'll stay in the car and read." I had no idea I was being set up by God. I pulled out a book I had brought along, *Visioneering* by Andy Stanley,[10] and as I read, these passages leapt out at me:

"When you look at the landscapes of your circumstances it is overwhelming. It just doesn't look like there is any way in the world to pull it off. That is always the case when God puts something on our hearts to do. The task always appears to be out of reach. God-ordained visions are always too big for us to handle. We shouldn't be surprised. Consider the source."

"There are always obstacles. There is always lack of resources. A man or woman with a vision usually feels alone, even isolated. Often there is little to go on other than gut-level, unquenchable, insatiable desire. And hopefully a sense of destiny: a feeling that this is what you were made for, an assurance that God has called you out into unchartered waters with a divine purpose in mind. If any of that rings true for you, you may be on the brink of something Divine."

By the time I finished these passages I was sobbing, and knew God was right there in the car with me, speaking prophetically to me and giving me answers to my questions. He wasn't done with me. I got a grip on my emotions and read further:

"His desire is to work through your circumstances to manoeuvre you into proper position…you don't know what God is up to behind the scenes of your life. You don't know how close you are to breakthrough. It is no accident that you are where you are. God is very much in control. God is using your circumstances to prepare you to accomplish His vision for your life. Your present circumstances are part of the vision. You are not wasting your time. You are not spinning your wheels. You are not wandering in the wilderness. If you are 'seeking first' His Kingdom where you are, then where you are is where He has positioned you." God was reaffirming to me His call and control over my life. I hadn't missed it! We weren't off course.

As I read on, I realized that I had the wrong measure of success, and why I had been in despair. Andy Stanley says, "Success is remaining faithful to the process God has laid out for you. ...Success is not the mile marker. Success is not the raise, the promotion, recognition, a Christian home or wonderful children. Those are simply enjoyable mile markers along the way. ...Unfortunately we don't often consider ourselves successful until we experience the rewards."

"You are a success every day you get up and show up for duty. Every day of faithfulness where you are there with what you have is a successful day...You are as successful now as you will be the day you see your vision materialize. If you measure your success by whether or not your vision has materialized, you are a candidate for discouragement. Confusing success with the rewards of success is one of the primary reasons people abandon their dreams."[10]

Those statements were like arrows going right to the centre of my being. He was so right; I was being tempted to abandon my vision because I wasn't measuring up to the false mile markers in my life. I thought of my husband who has been in ministry for over thirty years. I knew he didn't feel like a success many days, but he is faithful and determined to see God's purposes fulfilled in the Christian school where he works, and in the lives of the students. He is a success every day he shows up for duty. I spent an hour and fifteen minutes in that car having a one-on-one timeout with God. I came to see that my measure for success was distorted and ultimately unhealthy.

I am still humbled and clinging to the words of wisdom shared in that book. It was a powerful time. It helped me understand others who don't think they've been much of a success in God because things haven't gone according to their prophecies and the destiny they had expected.

Prophetic Vision for the Church

As people begin to step out into their destiny, we also want to see them find their place within a local church. Here is where the prophetic emphasis on service helps bring about alignment and unity.

I see many areas where we have only just begun in our local church. For example: children's prophetic ministry has only had seeds sown. I long for the day that someone will come along with heart geared towards the children and with a vision to develop their prophetic gifting. Another area that has been slower to develop corporately is a regular release of prophetic worship. Our worship teams are very sensitive to God's leading, and know how to help the congregation flow in praise and worship. What we want to see more regularly is unique expressions of God's heart through music and singing.

Several years ago one of our worship leaders received a public prophecy that she would be a songwriter, and that God would give her the songs prophetically. She was and is a great worship leader, but until that time had never even thought about song writing. After that word, God gave her songs specific to those who are broken and hurting, encouraging them that God is their Healer. In 2009 she released her first CD. I was particularly excited because it confirmed that prophecy is more than just a word of encouragement or direction. There is an impartation that empowers a person to actually realize the word. It's like the prophet Elijah lying on the widow's son and breathing life into him. The Holy Spirit has power through prophecy to breathe unfulfilled dreams and inspirations into being.

CHAPTER 14

MINISTRY INVOLVEMENT OF THE INTERMEDIATE & SENIOR TEAMS

The following are practical examples of how the Intermediate and Senior prophetic teams act as a resource for the local church. These are just some of the opportunities for ministry:

Graduations

As students graduate from our Christian school, we select a time where parents and friends can come to support them. A short teaching is done, mainly to the parents, on what the prophetic is about. The graduates have teaching ahead of time from one of the senior team members, as part of their regular classroom instruction.

We limit ministry to students from our church school. For a number of years we tried to include students within our congregation who were graduating from other schools, but that created problems we just could not overcome. It was easy to miss someone, even though we'd get a list of who was graduating from our youth pastor. Sometimes parents would come to us expecting their teenager to be prophesied over, even though the child never attended services or church activities. There was too much room for offense, so we simply offer it as a ministry privilege for those in our own Christian school.

Bible & Training School

Mission Trips—Students in their final year receive prophetic ministry just before they go out on a mission trip. This is a good time to build them up in their faith, identify some of their gifting, and impart a blessing to them.

Prophetic Teaching—Bible School students take a class about the prophetic. Mixing teaching with practical prophetic activity is a great way to equip students before they are involved in ministry. One former student has taken the concepts back to his home church 2,000 miles away, and is leading a ministry that teaches and trains prophetic people to serve their church community. That is a thrill for me (and my reward for teaching those early classes starting at 6:45 a.m. for many years, before I would go to work myself!)

Small Group Ministry

The Senior Team prophesies over the members of each Home Group (Small Group/House Church), as we are invited. Over the years, we have developed a formal process to prepare Home Group members for prophetic ministry. Hopefully, these details will assist you by enabling you to avoid many of the difficulties or problems we have already been challenged with.

Preparation: After receiving a request for ministry, I check with the church administrator, who helps oversee the Home Groups. We want to be sure the group is really ready to receive prophetic ministry (e.g. they shouldn't be new church members, the group should be well established, the leaders should have solid relationships with the group members, and be actively pastoring them). Approximately two weeks before the ministry night, a Senior Team member attends the house group meeting in order to present a teaching about prophecy. We have a standard format we use, which includes explaining what prophecy is, how to receive a prophetic word, and what to do with the word once it's given.

This teaching prior to the ministry is important, since we have new believers, as well as people from other churches, and those who may never have had any real understanding of the prophetic or prophetic in a home group setting. This pre-teaching requirement has helped us to avoid a lot of headaches and misunderstanding of what the prophetic will do for them. We have also compiled a set of guidelines that are sent out to the Home Group leaders, which the prophetic team member can also reinforce while they are doing the teaching.

Planning ahead with proper advance instruction to the small group will help avoid problems. Due to the nature of small groups being an informal setting, lack of preparation can leave you with an environment that feels chaotic and circus like. It can be very difficult to minister prophetically under such circumstances.

Example #1: One of the first groups we ministered to was made up of young families, and there were kids were running in and out of the room continually. Doors were slamming; one of the ministry team members couldn't concentrate. While we were ministering in the living room, he kept seeing kids running out onto the street and he was anxious that a child was going to get run over. We were not offered water nor anything to drink, and after three hours of ministry were getting worn out.

Now, before we schedule a time for prophetic ministry, I talk to the Home Group leaders about practical things such as: making arrangements for the children, setting a start and end time for the meeting, what to expect, and practical set-up. I may tell the leaders that we will need a break at a certain point. I check all of that ahead of time. Also, while we want the atmosphere to be relaxed and inviting, it is still important to remember that if you are asking God to speak, don't allow Him to be interrupted!

Example #2: A home group had requested prophetic ministry, and the Home Group leader was very evangelistic. The prophetic team had no idea ahead of time how many people would be there, but I planned for two groups of ministry—one upstairs and one down. People just kept coming into the groups for prophecy, and none of us knew where they were coming from. The leader, in his evangelistic style, had asked people to drop by his house. Some did not know God for sure, many had no church experience. Some would go downstairs for ministry and then come up to the other group for a second time through. It was bedlam and chaotic. We ministered from 7:00 until 11:00 p.m. While prophesying to people as an evangelistic tool is fantastic, those doing the prophecy must be prepared for that, and some type of order is always beneficial. After that experience we got a bit smarter and implemented the guidelines.

Helping Group Members to Have Proper Expectations of the Prophetic:

Prior to teaching, people sometimes have unhealthy expectations of the prophetic ministry. They may want God to speak to them about a specific area (a job, a relationship or ministry), and are disappointed when that isn't what they hear. Preparatory prayer and fasting shifts the onus onto what God wants to say, and not just a prayer for what they want to hear. They also begin to pray for those ministering. Some questions might be posed to the group: How much did I pray and prepare my heart for this ministry? Have I ever thought of what it is like to hear God's voice for other individuals? Have I ever thought of what it is like for these prophetic people to give up time in a busy schedule? Since implementing the preparatory teaching, we have had fewer issues with people being irritated with their prophetic word, or disappointed that a certain area wasn't addressed.

When people understand the teaching and criteria, it helps avoid unrealistic expectations for a specific prophetic word. If the Home Group is praying for those doing the ministry ahead of time, and even doing some fasting, a God-centred atmosphere for prophecy is created.

Who We Minister To:

People who regularly attend the house church and who have been members of the larger church for at least six months. We minister to couples together, but not to children.

Here is testimony from a leader whose Home Group was ministered to prophetically:

"Our house group decided to take advantage of HCC's well-developed prophetic ministry. So we invited the prophetic team to minister to the members of our house group. Diane Harrison and Brian Danchuk came and spent almost three hours prophesying over the members in our group.

This much anticipated evening was a great follow up to the focus on the prophetic at HCC. Group members were asked to review (our pastor) Joel's sermon on receiving the prophetic, and prepare through fasting and prayer. Some fasted from food, others from media. One even gave up coffee for three days!

The evening began with Todd Harrison, Diane's husband and an elder at HCC, anointing each member with oil and praying for healing. Every member of the group has been dealing with some form of long-term, chronic sickness, so this was a genuine blessing. This also set the tone for the remainder of the evening.

Diane and Brian then prophesied over each couple and the single members of the group individually. It was an amazing privilege to hear the words spoken over each person. We felt drawn closer together as a group and realized that we now had a fresh focus for future meetings. We also understand that we have a responsibility as a group to pray the prophetic into reality.... that we are each accountable for the words spoken over us. So in future meetings we will review our "words," and uphold each other in prayer. Our expectation is that over the coming months and years, we will be able to rejoice together as we see God's prophetic word come to pass in each of our lives." (Ranjan Thakre)

Prophetic ministry has been very positive for the Home Groups. Leaders say that it caused their group to be more strongly knitted together. There is a new respect for God's plan and authority in people's lives, as prophecy gives a larger God perspective. Prophesying in the home group setting is so effective because the group leaders are there as pastors, helping their people walk out the prophetic in their lives. Vision and passion are built into individuals' lives as they start hearing of God's desires and plans for their future. Sometimes, prophetic direction is identified for the group as a whole.

Example: "You are a very evangelistic group of people. God would have you reach out at every opportunity in the neighbourhood you are in. It is no accident that this group meets on the edge of the city's core community. You will be known and recognized for your good works and the trust will grow so that you have many opportunities to reach into the lives of the residents of this area." This prophecy was actually given to a Home Group that (unknown to those ministering) was planning a neighbourhood garage sale for the benefit of reaching the community, using the sale profits to be poured back into the community.

Other Small Group Ministry

We receive requests from other small groups for ministry at least a couple of times a year. Programs like 'Genesis' or 'Way of the Master' are intensive studies that usually require about a year of commitment and focus on spiritual growth. These are small groups of five to six people and are quite emotionally sensitive. I try to select prophetic people whose gifting will align those being ministered to. I would choose those who are gentle, more intercessory in prophetic style, and have the wisdom to present what they are seeing in a gracious manner. I don't want someone who is a real "truth" advocate calling down fire and brimstone on these folks while they are at a vulnerable and humble place. We strive to serve those we are ministering to. These are often people who have suffered life's bruising through abuse and neglect. Many times the people in the groups are broken. They remind me of the woman at the well with whom Jesus spent extra time, reassuring her that He had the living water that would become a spring within them. We try to model Jesus in these settings.

Missions Ministry

Our annual mission's conference is called Global Focus. We sponsor international, national and local ministries, and invite all of the leaders to our church to celebrate accomplishments and renew financial commitments for the coming year. In 2012 we had nine mission projects, with new ones on the horizon, as always. The three-day event has a very packed schedule, with celebration meals, cultural entertainment and time for Home Groups to connect with representatives of the ministries. In the midst of this, we schedule a couple of slots where these leaders receive prophetic ministry. The prophetic words are recorded, and many of the mission leaders use those recordings to keep themselves encouraged throughout the year. It is often a time in which they also receive confirmation about new directions, projects or territories they are planning to take on.

An individual who spent some time at our church and received prophetic ministry between services is now ministering in Africa, working with LeSEA Global Feed the Hungry. This is her testimony of prophetic encouragement: "My summer was a time of transition, and quite difficult. So often I would listen to the prophetic words that were spoken over me when I had been at Harvest City, because they were life-giving! I am so thankful for that time of ministry. I truly feel that was the main purpose God brought me there!"

Referral Prophetic Ministry

During times when our church association, "LifeLinks," gathers its leaders, our pastors will often refer these leaders for prophetic ministry. They will attend the 'between-service ministry' for such things as counselling, or advising about church strategy and growth. At those times, much of the prophetic ministry provides confirmation of plans made in other meetings. One person asked, "Were you in the room when we were planning strategy yesterday? The prophecy you have spoken lines up exactly with what we were discussing!"

In 2011 during a youth convention, one of the pastors from another city asked for prophetic ministry for himself and his youth team. There were about eight people. In contrast to the Home Group ministry, these sessions are usually quite informal. I invite three or four members from the Senior Team; we open up with prayer, and then as God leads, begin to prophesy about the directions or purposes of their local church, God's plans for their community, and for individuals themselves. The church was really encouraged with that ministry, and is now in correspondence with me about how to start building their own prophetic team. (That pastor was one of several contacts, including one from China, which I received during a four-week period prior to God speaking to me about writing this book. So the encouragement was reciprocal.)

Participation of the Team Members

Involving all of the team members as much as possible is very important, both for their own development and for prophetic ministry within and outside of the church. Leaders must be conscious of the need to replace themselves. I often wonder: "if I was out of the picture for whatever reason, how much of the ministry built up over the years would stand?" If you find someone who can lead and teach, nurture them. Resist the urge to do all the teaching yourself. It is important to prepare other leaders who have both the gifting and passion to train others in the prophetic. They need to be convinced of the value of the prophetic to change people's lives, love the presence of God, and be able to lead people, while modelling the faith required for stepping out in prophecy.

CHAPTER 15

REGULAR PROPHETIC MINISTRY TO THE CHURCH
(MINISTRY BETWEEN SERVICES)

There was a time when most of our congregation had no real connection to the prophetic. New people were coming to the church all the time, and their only frame of reference for the prophetic was hearing someone give a prophetic word during a Sunday service. I felt that the prophetic was not relevant to most of the congregation, and the prophetic teams were not nearly accessible enough. As well, most of our prophetic team members did not have enough opportunity to minister, so it seemed like a perfect match. We got the idea (suggested during our Senior Team meetings) to host prophetic ministry—available to everyone, on Sundays—in between our two services. We knew that it would be challenging; we had only thirty minutes between services. Then on a broader scope was the challenge of sustaining such a ministry in a beneficial way on a long term basis. This undertaking would require commitment and order.

The results, however, were worth the effort, and have been nothing short of incredible, as the congregation is individually encouraged and lifted up by God Himself, through the words of the prophetic teams. The prophetic has become established and strong, bringing life to the church.

Timing

I do not recommend that anyone embark on a ministry like this unless you have trained prophetic people. This type of ministry should only be engaged once you have started a prophetic team, and have people ready to offer balanced, consistent prophetic words that bring increased comfort, exhortation and edification to peoples' lives—not confusion. Do not attempt to implement this too early in your journey of developing prophetic people, as you won't be able to maintain it. It is important to ensure that there are sufficient prophetic resources, willing to go the distance with such an endeavour. You do not want it to become one more example of people having high hopes of the prophetic, and then being left disappointed when it drops off. We have learned from our many ministry experiences some important keys for implementation of regular prophetic ministry.

How it Works

We have two Sunday morning services, so our ministry time is scheduled between the two services. This allows only thirty minutes for the entire process, so organization and promptness from all involved, as well as advance set-up is required. (If you have only one service, you could arrange a pre or post-service session.)

People wanting to receive prophetic ministry come to a designated room in the church promptly at 10:30 when the first service ends. This allows each ministry group about three sets of people to minister to for a maximum of ten minutes each (and that is a stretch for some of them). They can't really handle more ministry than three groupings without a break. People sign in and leave their contact information at a table outside the ministry room. They are then ushered into the ministry room to a selected "ministry station." There are four stations set-up in the same large room. They are called in on a first-come, first-serve basis.

- We allocate ten minutes per person or couple for prophetic ministry. Ten minutes is adequate time for someone to receive an encouraging word.

- A team of three, one Senior person and two others take turns prophesying.

- The prophetic words are recorded on hand held digital recorders. Those receiving ministry will have their recorded prophecy emailed to them in approximately one week. They are free to share their recording with whomever they like, or just keep it for their own reference.

Set up & Structure of the Ministry

We offer ministry between services every first and third Sunday of the month. We have six Senior Team members, so we have three ministry teams per Sunday; that way each Senior Team member is only scheduled once a month. It's a perfect ministry arrangement for the intermediate level or more junior people, since three people minister in a group; that way if they don't have a word to give every time, it's not a problem. Usually the intermediate people have shorter prophecies, and feel more confident when they have a Senior person there with them. The Prophetic Leader or Coordinator does the scheduling and makes the arrangements. The ministry occurs in a large room with a few teams ministering at separate stations. There are a few reasons why I believe that one large room is best:

- As the co-ordinator, I want to be able to oversee what is happening both with the ministry teams and the people coming in to be ministered to. If we had people go to four separate rooms for ministry, I would be unable, at a glance, to keep my eye on what was going on. This is important in order to help keep things running smoothly and troubleshoot any problems.

- It is more time-consuming for the check-in person to take people to a separate room for ministry

It does take discipline to shut out the other people speaking in the room and concentrate on prophesying. Having big separations between groups is best. I have the chairs set up so that the people ministering speak towards the corners of the room, so that hopefully the walls absorb the sound. It seems to work well. (Portable sound panels of some kind could also be used.)

If one group is finished before the ten minute time-frame, additional people are brought in. On the other hand, if there is a person being ministered to who wants to keep talking or give the team feedback, I'll escort them out or bring in a new person to be ministered to, and escort the person who has already received ministry out. This has happened on a few occasions. I understand that people are excited about the word they have received, but they can talk to the prophetic ministers at a later time, or fill in the feedback sheet. The big picture is to keep the ministry times as efficient as possible.

The Ministry Workers

Getting the right people for the tasks takes some thought. Try to utilize people who don't have too many other responsibilities. I select the workers and book them in about a week before the ministry time. I find that if I book too far in advance, people forget, but I have very few cancellations when I book just a week in advance. After two years, I still have people volunteering to minister. (Sometimes there are people vying for the position.) I track who is on the ministry team and try to be fair in selecting people. Each member of the team ministers once every one to two months. The ones that have grown in their gift and are deemed trustworthy will be put in charge of a team of three. Remember: prophetic people need to prophesy!

Everyone on the team has either had prophetic training at the Intermediate level or has just completed the Introductory sessions and is awaiting Intermediate level classes. People are asked to be on a ministry team by invitation, so if I see someone with a strong gift in the introductory class times, I will ask them at the end of the training to come and minister on a team. I try to put them in a ministry group with me so I can mentor and encourage them.

Over time I notice that those who have less gifting aren't comfortable being on a team. Some just don't have the level of gifting required. Yes, they can still prophesy and be a blessing in other ways, but they aren't people who I would say have a true "prophetic ministry," and often they have other gifts that are stronger than prophecy.

When people come to help with the ministry, I assign them their team that day, give a bit of instruction and open with a prayer for our ministry time. I also remind people of a few guidelines:

- Keep prophecy in the realm of comfort, edification or exhortation.
- Remember, prophecy is only one tool God uses in people's lives.
- Don't spend time counselling people. Refer them to our pastoral and counselling staff.
- Encourage people to fill out the feedback forms.
- Avoid saying things like "I don't know if this from God or not." (creates mistrust or uneasiness in the receiver).

The Check-in Person: This person sits at a table in the hallway outside the ministry room. To run a successful ministry requires a check-in person with the following attributes/skills:

- Good communication skills; need to be friendly, and be able to introduce themselves.
- Ability to be efficient in getting people signed in and obtaining their contact information. Keep cool under pressure. A lot happens in a short time.

- Ability to be assertive enough to explain the ground rules to people. Example: Order: First come/First served; Session over-booked: ask people to return next time ministry is available. They may also have to explain that we don't prophesy over children or that we cannot minister to a family of four as a single unit. (All actual examples.)
- Good perception / sense of where the person might be from (church member, brand-new to the church, hesitant person).

The actual work performed by the check in person includes:

- Greet people, sign them in, and obtain their contact information.
- Offer an information sheet on the prophetic.
- Seat people in the waiting area, and let them know how long they might expect to wait.

The Overseer

I act as overseer for this operation. As much as possible I am on a ministry team, but I'm also overseeing the flow of people in and out. The check-in person is trained to maintain the flow of people in and out of the ministry room. I troubleshoot if someone at the check-in table needs a more assertive approach. I'm always in motion during this thirty minute ministry time, and feel the need to be strong and direct with people, as I am concerned with the big picture of the ministry. I don't want people backed up down the hall waiting unnecessarily, nor do I want big waitlists for the next Sunday's ministry time. I make sure that I always have two strong people on my ministry team as I will often prophesy over the person at my station, then leave or tell the team to go ahead without me as I sort out the check-in area.

It was prophesied over me years before we started with this ministry that I would be like a Mother Superior training the younger nuns, giving orders and directives. Almost every week that I'm in the room for this ministry, my mind goes back to that prophecy. That's exactly who I feel like—Mother Superior!

Digital Recordings

The ministry relies on a person with technical skills to download the prophetic words from a digital audio recorder and to ensure that the prophecy is emailed or a CD provided to the right person. This is why the sign-in process is so important. We want to ensure that we have accurate and complete contact information. We record the full name of the person being prophesied over on the digital recorder at the start of their session. Sometimes this gets forgotten, in which case we do it at the end of the session before they leave. This process makes it easy for the recording to be matched to the individuals contact information and sent to them in a timely manner. This is a volunteer position requiring patience and perseverance. Sometimes it's not easy to decipher peoples writing or their requests such as: "send an email to my friend's computer," (completely different name) or "leave a CD in my church mailbox."

This is totally a behind-the-scenes ministry. The person who sends the recording also includes a feedback sheet, so that we can hear how we are doing in the ministry. To date, I have had three people volunteer in this capacity, and they all had vision for the prophetic. The ones who stay with it are secure in their calling that this is an important and valuable ministry. Those wanting more public recognition, leave.

Advertising & Promoting the Ministry

We do this in several ways. The ministry is promoted in the church bulletin and on a monthly calendar. From time to time we put an insert into the bulletin. Sometimes an individual requests ministry directly from a member of the prophetic team or church leadership in advance, in which case they are asked to select a scheduled date and then show up. Our pastor and leaders endorse the ministry from the pulpit, although that occurs less frequently now, since it has become established.

Initially, we were afraid that we'd have a stampede if it was promoted from the pulpit, so we quietly slipped a notice into the bulletin, then just made an announcement that day during church that prophetic ministry was available between services. Even with this low-key approach, we still have people arriving at 10:00 a.m. to receive ministry, and by 10:30 there's usually a line-up.

I have had the opportunity to speak on Sunday to teach about the prophetic, providing examples of how this ministry is impacting lives. It is beneficial to bring understanding to the congregation regarding why we prophesy, and the value for the church as a whole, and individually.

Accountability and Dealing with Complaints

Every person receiving ministry gets a copy of the prophetic word and this allows a great opportunity to deal with any complaints or misunderstandings. We have had very few problems. I recently reviewed a recording in which the senior minister on the team thought the junior member had been harsh in prophesying over a young adult who was new to the church. When I reviewed it, there was much spoken to the recipient about being self-critical and being hard on herself. I thought the senior person had misunderstood, and I didn't agree that it was a harsh word. I did have a pastor follow up with this recipient to see if there was a problem. Thankfully there wasn't. Sometimes I review a tape because I'm interested in hearing the team members gifting and how they are handling themselves. If the person receiving prophecy is part of a Small Group, we notify the leader that this person received prophetic ministry. The intent is to strengthen communication with the group leader, and give them an opportunity to follow up in a pastoral way with that person.

Results—How it's Going

Complaints: In the first year of operation I had one single complaint. I was told people ministering took too long praying before they started to prophesy, and that the prophecy was on a surface level. The complaint was somewhat valid, but again people need to have a little more grace with those prophesying. The great thing about the between-service ministry is that I can go back and listen to the recording, and then give input to the complainant, and guidance to those who prophesied, if they need it.

In our second year, the biggest problem was that people went beyond comfort, edification and encouragement into directional prophecy or inaccurate interpretations. I need to reinforce to the people ministering that we are offering prophecy that is not judgemental, harsh or directional. For example, we would consider it too harsh to say, "There is sin in your life," or too directional to say, "God wants you to move to another 'particular' city." Our experience is that God provides direction and correction in a direct and personal communication with people as they take hold of the prophetic word they receive. The Holy Spirit moves beyond our words into the hearts of men and women.

After the first year and a half of between-service ministry, we had to make a few adjustments for efficiency's sake. For instance, we have to tell people not to bring their children. You might think this is just common sense, but people have to be told. We can't be babysitting while a parent is receiving ministry. We also have the set minimum age guidelines of eighteen years. Parents must consent if there is a child seeking ministry. We limit the number of people being ministered to at a single station. We don't want someone bringing themselves and their five kids for ministry. In most cases two is the maximum number we will accommodate per station. This can be a couple or a parent and child; however the preference is for individual ministry. We also have to tell people not to come if they've had prophecy within the last six months. This allows us to offer ministry to a broader segment of the congregation. I had to tell the prophetic team to give deference to the congregation, as some of them were coming in to receive ministry if they weren't on a team.

We have already ministered to hundreds during this between-service ministry. As a result we expect to see people in the congregation more encouraged, and operating with greater faith and vision to carry out what God has called them to. Imagine what it will look like in another three years? Five years?

We have had very good feedback. Here are just a couple of examples:

One man was brought to the prophetic ministry by a friend. He was a skeptic, at least on the surface. Our young adults leader began to prophesy to him describing the country where had just spent eight years and describing the job he was doing while he was there. He was so shaken up that he had to get his friend to take him outside and walk around the church building. This experience caused him to re-examine the direction his life was going and to get serious about God.

At one session, I prophesied over a young woman. The words were so basic, about the love God had for the one sheep, and how He never meant for us to walk alone. I asked if she had ever invited God to have a personal relationship with her. She hadn't but was so open. She prayed to receive the Lord. I believe it was a sincere commitment and she was primed and ready for that step. To me, the comfort, edification and exhortation became only a bonus, or a means for her coming to faith in Christ. Pastors love it when they see people being ministered to, provided with the encouragement and hope, and spurred on to faith so that they can overcome their problems. To see people added to the church through the gift of prophecy and the Holy Spirit at work is downright exciting, and helps all ministries realize that they are working together to extend the Kingdom of God.

A Pastor's Perspective

This type of prophetic ministry really makes a difference to the entire church—pastors, leaders, and congregation. Following is a note from our pastor, which will provide you with a hint of the impact made by having a prophetic team:

"To Intermediate/Senior Prophetic Teams and all who do the between service ministry:

Over a year ago when Diane Harrison pitched her vision for the between service ministry of the prophetic team, I was excited about the possibilities of this. It seemed like a great opportunity to both minister to the congregation while at the same time give more opportunity for the Intermediate Team to grow and develop in their gifting. That was the goal that was in mind.

After more than a year now of this ministry being in operation, I was just thinking of how successful this venture has been, and how blessed we have been as a church to have this ministry. I want to personally take this opportunity to thank each and every one of you for your service to the Lord in this way. I have talked to so many people who have told me how blessed they have been by the ministry and I have heard of and seen many of you growing in your gifting. There have been several times before service, in pre-prayer, when I personally have received a word from one of you that has blessed me so much.

I believe that God has called us as a church to raise up prophetic ministers who minister with accuracy, but most importantly from a heart that wants to serve and bless the body. I want to encourage you to keep this heart and to keep pushing into the prophetic and stretching yourself. We need to hear the voice of God as a church and our people need to have the vision, healing, encouragement and impartation that the prophetic word brings to their life. I'm praying and believing God that we are going to go even deeper in this ministry this year.

You are doing a great job!
Joel Wells
Lead Pastor, Harvest City Church

CHAPTER 16

PROPHETIC EVANGELISM

"It was Jesus' modus operandi to demonstrate God's power to someone and then explain it. He used the word of knowledge, the word of wisdom and prophecy to cause people to reflect about their lives. Approaching people with positive feedback from the Holy Spirit will get their attention and it may open the door to further discussion about Jesus and the supernatural." Prophecy, Dreams and Evangelism, Doug Addison[11].

Twenty years ago, when we began our journey in the prophetic, we did not see this aspect to our ministry. Now it has become an exciting part of our prophetic ministry.

Outreach Opportunities: As an offshoot of the prophetic evangelism classes we began to offer other teaching sessions on evangelism, planning and outreaches. These classes weren't limited to the prophetic team people, but they did make up about two-thirds of the group. The sessions were offered regularly in the spring, in order to gear up for summer outreaches.

One of our Senior Team Members headed up a booth during our city's annual fair—an event attracting tens of thousands of people to the fairgrounds of our city.

This is our prophetic booth story: We used an evangelism program, including draws and giveaways to invite people to come and take what we titled, "The Good Test." We decided to add a separate prophetic station and do "spiritual readings" in a booth called "Know Your Destiny." We wanted it generic enough that we would not just attract Christians.

As soon as people came to the booth, we established that we were neither psychics nor fortune tellers, but were Christians, with God as our source and inspiration. Our booth was jammed in with the hundreds of other vendors selling everything from rug cleaners to jewellery. There were several booths offering "spiritual guidance," including a palm reader, a psychic who did a platform show every two hours, and other new age venues. In the midst of all that, we proceeded to prophesy and minister to the broken and lost. Young people and aboriginal people were the most frequent guests, and at times there was standing room only.

Brian, from our Senior Team, had taken a week off work to give himself to overseeing the booth. My husband, Todd, and I were moving that summer, so I was there for three partial days. It was a fantastic experience! I've never felt so much like Jesus in the marketplace in my life, and I believe that we made an impact. Some people who came were at such a low point that I don't think they'd still be alive had they not received a word of hope and encouragement.

One aboriginal man was so humble when he came in and sat down. He took off his cowboy hat and said he'd grown up in a residential school with a history of sexual abuse, and had tried everything to ease the resulting pain—drugs, alcohol, etc.—but it always came back. He asked if we could help him. We prayed and prophesied, and trust that God put seed of hope in his heart. I believe that prophetic impartation saved his life that day.

There were some powerful divine encounters. It was very hard on Brian, as the booth was open from 10 a.m. in the morning until 11:00

or 12:00 at night, and the rules for securing a booth in the fair required us to man it throughout the entire time the doors were open. We not only felt that the booth was a huge success, but it was also a milestone for our prophetic teams to take on such a challenge.

The next year, I did the coordination for the booth with a Senior prophetic person assigned to oversee all the time periods that the booth was open. We worked in shifts of three to four hours. The annual fair is the last week of July and/or first week of August, which is the prime holiday week in our province, so it was certainly not easy to fill all of the shifts. Twenty people had already planned a mission trip to northern Saskatchewan. Many people could only do one three-hour shift. It took 40 people to man that booth, plus the Senior Prophetic people, so it was a huge organizational feat—getting everyone tickets to enter the fairgrounds, continual changes to the schedule, etc. In spite of all the hard work, the effort was worth it. People wanted us to return the following year. Countless people from the church were trained and stretched in prophetic evangelism. It was a fantastic time for people to begin to see how the prophetic can be highly relevant in day-to-day life.

On the other hand, it was a lot for the Senior Team to carry, as the volunteers for ministry weren't always the strongest prophetically; therefore the Senior Team had to be prepared to carry the weight of prophesying. I loved it as a training experience, because people who came for ministry were very direct and they would just say, "No, I don't think that was right about my friend, but what she said to me is right on. How do you guys do this stuff?" Our people had to be prepared to hear that their prophetic gift wasn't as accurate as they thought it was.

I was working at the booth one night with a young couple, and we'd had some people who had been there earlier, and came back with other family members to be ministered to. It was an aboriginal family from out of town, and they were blessed by the words they were receiving.

When the couple was done prophesying over the older man, this grandpa of the group turned to me and said, "I want to hear what you will say over me." The young couple had already spent about twenty minutes prophesying over him so I said, "No way, you have had your turn; we have others to minister to." (I felt it was important to validate the young couple, and wanted to demonstrate that I was absolutely confident in their abilities to hear from God.) Now if that had been a church setting, someone would likely have walked away offended, but this was the world and it was free ministry. That man just laughed his head off when I said no, he couldn't try out everyone in the booth for a word. People are so interesting.

We continue to be involved in prophetic evangelism, and the outreach areas are still going strong. We didn't do the fairground ministry after the second year mainly because of the heavy commitment required by so many. Besides that, my husband, who is wholly supportive of my ministry involvement, wanted me to take the summer off. He wanted a normal wife and a normal summer for once, one where we didn't have to plan our summer rejuvenation around ministry commitments. This is the man who has seen me travel to the Philippines, Taiwan and other ministry trips, praying and fasting for me while I'm away. So when he wanted me at home, I felt it was only fair.

Instead we had prophetic people sign up to work at the evangelism booth. I personally can't do their style of evangelism. I can't ask people if they've ever told a lie, and then, when they admit they have, look them in the eye and tell them that means they're a liar. I would turn beet red from embarrassment. So I would just be in the evangelism booth, and when they went through the salvation prayer with people, the leader would ask me if I had anything to add. I would sit the person down and prophesy God's heart of love towards them. I love the fact that there is room in our church for diverse streams of thought and ministry to work together. I have quite strong feelings about that style of evangelism, but it does seem to work for some people, so I can just keep my opinions to myself and flow with what I can do.

Treasure Hunts

What is a Treasure Hunt? ibethel.org[12] website describes them this way:

"Treasure Hunts incorporate the use of words of knowledge (clues) that you write on your Treasure Map to find Treasures (people) who need a supernatural encounter with God through an encouraging prophetic word or healing. This is not about preaching or arguing with people, but rather giving them a practical demonstration of the goodness of God. Treasure hunts are a great tool for those who have felt intimidated by witnessing to family members, friends, co-workers and those in the community. Through this fun and easy method, you become empowered with confidence and competence to bring supernatural encounters to people around you. Through treasure hunts you can become a world changer, transforming your community one encounter at a time!"

Some members of the prophetic teams initiated Treasure Hunts on a regular basis. Here are a couple of their stories:

Biker testimony:

"One particular night, while spending time asking God for clues, I sensed I was supposed to go Tim Horton's, a popular coffee shop in the north end of our city. The clues I received about people's appearance were: blond hair, green eyes, black jacket and huge hoodie. I also felt one of the areas I was supposed to pray for was emotional healing. There were two others guys who also felt they should go to Tim Horton's, so off we went.

When we arrived, the place was packed. The boys lined up for coffee, and I found the last table in the place. I looked over and saw a nearby table full of bikers. Even from just glancing at them, I felt the Holy Spirit pull at me, and I knew I was supposed to share with them.

My first response was, "Oh no Lord, I'm not ready to take this big of a risk yet! Where is a cute, harmless, elderly couple having coffee that I could talk to?"

When a few bikers got up to go smoke, I saw three of them had blond hair (later I saw their green eyes). One of the women had a black jacket on and another woman wore a huge hoodie covered with skulls. These matched my clues. I knew God wanted to do something at this table.

When the boys arrived with the coffee, I told them I was supposed to talk with the table of bikers. "What do I have to lose? Except for my life," I joked.

I finally worked up my courage, went over and introduced myself. The whole group looked at me like: "What are you doing here?"

I explained that I was with a group who believes in a very real God, and we make ourselves available to see if there are people God wants us to talk to and pray for. Then I read the list of clues I felt God gave me about the appearance of the people He wanted me to minister to.

"Hey, that's our table right here," one of the guys said.

"I know!" I replied, "So is there anything that I can pray for you guys about?"

They laughed because they had all been in motorcycle accidents and their bodies were pretty beat up. A few were in serious enough accidents they should have died. Two were left with serious brain injuries and were unable to work.

I asked one of the women with a brain injury if I could pray for her because God wanted to heal her. She said sure. At this point, most were very cautious and a couple were staring daggers at me. But as I prayed for her, the Holy Spirit fell and I sensed His presence strongly at the table. The woman began to cry as I asked God to heal her. When I finished praying, I asked if there was any way to test if she was healed, but she said no. I don't know if God healed her, but I definitely know He was doing something in her.

The man with her then spoke up saying he was in three bike accidents and after the third, something unusual happened that he hadn't been able to share with anyone in this biker gang. After his third accident, Jesus appeared to him in a dream, giving him a Scripture verse. When he awoke, he was totally freaked out and found a Bible, and sure enough the verse was in there.

So he tracked down members of a Christian bike gang in the city, and they introduced him to the chaplain. He told the chaplain about the dream and asked what it meant. The chaplain said this Scripture meant God wants to change his life and use him to draw others to God.

I asked this fellow if he gave his life to the Lord when all this happened. He said, "Yes," and that it had totally changed him.

I then turned to the biggest guy and asked if I could pray for him. He said "Sure," and said basically everything was fine except his right arm which was damaged in an accident. I prayed for him and asked if there was any way of testing if he was healed. He said he felt fine then, but he would know in a few minutes if there was still pain. I said if he feels any more pain that I would pray for him again because God wants to heal him.

I then turned to one of the other girls at the table. She was one of the two who didn't look happy that I was there. I prophesied a word God had for her in the area of emotional healing. She began to cry, as I believe God was doing something in her. But after the word, she wouldn't let me pray for her. I said that was totally fine, and added that I hoped during her journey, she finds God and lets him take away her pain, because it wasn't how the Lord wanted her to live.

"I know that was really strange," I told the group as I was leaving, "but I just feel God wanted you to know that He loves you and that He's thinking about you."

It was obvious from the direction God gave us and the dream given one of the bikers, the Lord wanted to minister to this group. When I walked away, I was overwhelmed by how God had shown up, and realized if I hadn't been willing to take this risk, it wouldn't have happened like that."

Money Testimony:

"On one of our treasure hunt nights, I went out with a girl named Kelsey. We decided to go to the mall, and as we were walking up to the entrance, Kelsey asked me what my clues were. I had written down: woman, short dark hair, and facial piercing like a nose ring. As I told Kelsey what clues I had, we walked right past a girl in the entrance way with that exact description. I knew she was the right one because when you learn to recognize God's voice or leading, you get those kind of butterflies or sick feeling when you know you're supposed to do something, or that's who you're looking for.

Anyway, I just stopped her and said, "I know you don't know me and might think this is crazy, so no pressure at all. But I'm just with my friend and we're going around seeing if there are any people that we feel like God wants us to talk to or pray for." Then I showed her my paper where I had written down the clues that were like her appearance, and she was excited and said, "Hey that's me!" I didn't have any direction on where to go from there, so I asked her if there anything we could pray for her about. She said no, but that she just wanted us to pray.

The pressure was on because I had *no* idea what to even pray for. But I just took a second to hear from God and He gave me some words of knowledge about her past. She was clearly being affected as I was talking about these events, but then I said, "Because of all of this that you have gone through, you feel like God is against you. But God wants you to know how much He loves you, and I feel like He is going to begin to bless you even financially, so that you know He is for you, and not against you. I feel like random people are going to come to you and begin to give you money. Or co-workers and friends are going to begin to give you things, like even extra food they've cooked or baking, etc. God is going to bless you financially so you know He is with you."

Now we always pray with our eyes open so we don't seem weird, and so we can see what's going on around us. As I was just saying the part about random people coming to give her money, I saw a woman burst through the entrance doors. I didn't even think she saw us because she seemed focused on what she was doing. She walked to the bank machine, took out money, walked over and gave the money to my friend Kelsey, and walked away.

Just as I finished prophesying, Kelsey handed the money to the woman we were praying for and, said, "Umm, that woman just came and said, 'Give this money to Penny'." We looked down, and the woman we were praying for had a name tag on and it said 'Penny'.

So picture it: as I literally just finish saying, 'Random people are going to come give you money,' this woman comes out of nowhere and gives

Kelsey money to give to Penny. Penny didn't know who the woman was who gave her the money, and the woman just walked away after giving Kelsey the money, and was gone. The three of us stood there stunned. The woman we were praying for (Penny) was in total shock, and all I said was, "Umm, even we are a bit freaked out right now, but all I can say is that God just *really* wants you to know He loves you."

We don't see things like this happening every time we go out on our Treasure Hunts. Sometimes people turn us down or they don't get healed when we pray. But we keep stepping out and pushing into the life we believe God has called us to live as His disciples.

Because I believe 'He is who He says He is', I will continue to make myself available to impact people's lives as He has impacted mine."

Megan Reves, Senior Prophetic Team member
Harvest City Church

CHAPTER 17

PROPHETIC MINISTRY
FOR CHILDREN

Many children raised in environments where the Holy Spirit is free to work can be led into prophecy very naturally and easily, because they respond from their hearts and spirits rather than their minds. Working with the leader of children's ministry is a good way to introduce exercises for kids. There is a certain amount of creativity needed. In our Christian school, one teacher asked the children if they had a prophetic word to give. The classroom was completely silent. She then asked if anyone saw any pictures or felt God was showing them something. Immediately, they began to describe their pictures and who it was meant for. Example: "I saw Clinton fishing from a boat and he was pulling in fish and more fish etc...." It's clear that children have the ability and simple faith to step into a prophetic revelation if they are given the right coaching and environment.

Many Sunday school teachers are not aware of, and few are actually trained in the prophetic. I believe this a huge missed opportunity. I occasionally lead teaching sessions with the volunteer Sunday school teachers, so they can help me when I do prophetic exercises with large groups of children. This is an area that could really be developed. I am so looking forward to the day someone steps up to the plate with a heart to lead and train children in this way. I believe that those trained young in the prophetic will be a mighty, powerful force for the glory of God.

If you have prophetic people with a heart for training children, *let them at it!* Give them whatever help or encouragement they need to get moving in this area. Receiving training while young is *invaluable!*

CHAPTER 18

PROPHETIC ARTS EXPRESSION

Prophetic arts cannot be easily defined, but when you see the prophetic in these areas, no one has to tell you it's prophetic. You know, in the same way your spirit witnesses to a prophetic word. It can be a very powerful reflection of the heart of God. I believe that I have seen what could truly be defined as prophetic art.

I was visiting another church, and as the worship began a man was off to the side painting. His painting was of a beautiful open church-like window, and you could see light pouring through it and reaching a lost community. As he was painting, people began to prophesy about God's heart for the community. There was a clear connection between the painting and the prophetic words, and it had a positive impact on the entire service.

Occasionally, we have used an art expression activity as part of a prophetic team meeting. We gave each person the name of someone who had a need for healing, then worked on some personal prophetic pictures and poetry for those sick people. One time the whole activity was focused on a young woman suffering from cancer, whose illness was so severe that she was confined to her house. We gathered up all the art and poetry and took it to her. She was able to keep these tokens of God's love and encouragement close to her. It was a powerful, practical use of the gifts.

I spent some time working with the woman who was overseeing arts, in effort to assist her in identifying prophetic expression within the arts, and showing how to create a team environment with purposeful goals. She learned how to train up a team, and how to communicate and structure what the artists do in order to be a benefit to the church. She has the grace to work with this group. For me, it would have been a disaster to try to take on such a task, because I had no vision for leading it. Sometimes the best thing is to say "No," and to know yourself well enough to be aware of what you have grace and ability to do, and what you don't. My husband has remarked numerous times after hearing me on the phone to a prophetic person that he can't believe how I handled the situation without reacting, and also with wisdom. That's because God has given me grace for that which I'm destined to do, and I can't pretend to be something else, or someone I'm not.

I was inspired to ask the leader of the arts team to participate in the Sunday between-services prophetic ministry. She came to the session with her canvasses and paints. As others on the team ministered prophetically, she painted a picture and then gave the interpretation. I was excited to see this practical demonstration of art in a prophetic environment. One person who came for ministry had been released on a day-pass from psychiatric treatment. As he was being ministered to, tears flowed down his face. When he left, he had a prophetic picture to take with him which would remind him of the encouragement God gave him at the session. It was wonderful to see how God uses each one in his/her own gifting for the building up of the Kingdom.

Prophetic props or actions are also a useful and valid prophetic expression. A Senior Team member who worked in an army surplus store brought in various army props and used them as part of a prophecy. We have repeated this approach at different times using a variety of props. A helmet, swords, shields, torches, tent pegs all can be related to prophetic themes for individuals or groups.

One of the strongest prophetic pictures that I can remember was when Rachel Hickson, an international speaker from England, came to our church. She positioned our pastors and elders on-stage in an arrow pattern. She was very specific about where each person should stand, and then she prophesied about their position in the arrow and how they were to function within the church. Any time a picture can be used, whether in words or props, the message is enhanced, helping people remember it.

You have to exercise some caution with artistic expression, as it can easily become self-indulgent. This gets very sensitive, because it is a judgement call. While it is subjective, it is a leader's responsibility to exercise appropriate judgement.

YOU HAVE TO EXERCISE SOME CAUTION WITH ARTISTIC EXPRESSION, AS IT CAN EASILY BECOME SELF-INDULGENT.

Prophetic arts ministry is about much more than performance. Artistic expression during worship should always *be* worshipful to and *cause* worship to our God. In no way do we want to draw any attention away from worshipping our God. Truly prophetic art expression brings ministry to a person or a group of people from God. It is intended to serve the church and help people to grow and develop in their relationship with God. As with prophetic words, we don't interrupt the flow of a service or worship time inappropriately.

The arts have a unique way of cutting through the walls that people often erect around their hearts, allowing God's message to penetrate even the most hardened characters. The arts can turbo-charge prophecy, serve to impart grace, and empower people to fulfill the prophetic vision for their lives.

"...there are things God wants to communicate in the earth that will never come to fullness without the yielding of creative people—artists who know they are prophetic and desire to release through the arts." Matt Tommey, theworshipstudio.blogspot.ca[13]

CHAPTER 19

PROPHETIC WORSHIP
(INCLUDING PROPHETIC SONG & PROPHECY WITH INSTRUMENTS)

This is an area on which entire books are written, but because it is such an important aspect of the gift of prophecy, I wanted to include just a few thoughts on the subject:

I think it is the ultimate gift when a prophetic person has the ability to sing or play an instrument with the song of the Lord, as an option to simply speaking out the Word of the Lord. Many times, hearts can be melted through this medium—more so than through words alone. I believe that bondages can be broken, and people set free through the anointing of prophetic song and prophetic worship. We see a Biblical example expressed in the Old Testament when Saul calls for David the minstrel to come and play, in order to drive the evil spirits away.

In teaching prophetic teams, we discuss prophetic song and prophecy with instruments as one of the ways God speaks to us. We incorporate related definitions into the teaching material, in a similar way to how we describe God using visions, dreams, and impressions.

Prophetic song is "song that is inspired, anointed and directed by the Holy Spirit through an individual, usually spontaneous in nature, which expresses the mind of God in musical form. It is literally prophecy through song. These songs are directed to man for the purpose of edification, exhortation and comfort or may be directed to God as the Holy Spirit helps us express our deep devotion that we could not ordinarily express by ourselves." Hamon[14]

The function of the prophetic team meeting is not to raise up prophetic worshippers (it may be a wonderful by-product), but if people understand the use of their gift through prophetic song, it can be a foundational seed leading them in that direction. It is the same for prophetic arts. We see this as a valid communication of God's thoughts, ideas and purposes, but the team meetings only validate the prophetic expression of the gift—we don't teach the skill development of art, dance etc.

In its most basic definition, prophetic worship is "speaking, singing or acting under the influence of the Spirit of the Lord which in turn, shows our complete surrender in worship to Him (God). Prophetic worship is meant to allow God's reflection to be seen in us so that others may respond and come to know Him.

"....Prophetic worship is a way to live life so that God's heart, words and voice are made obvious to those around us." theworship-studio.blogspot.ca[15]

My friend, Margaret Graham, from Harvest Church, Calgary, Alberta, has recorded and raised up many prophetic worship teams. She has this to say:

"God gives us the power to see into people's live and situations. As we lead, our worship should meet people right where they are in their lives. Every time we sing a song together, all the people should feel as though that song was written specifically for them. As a lead worshipper I spend time looking for songs that are not just personally moving, but corporately challenging.

As I prepare by praying and worshipping on my own, it is much easier to hear the voice of God "in the moment." It is often those "in the moment" times, when we are not distracted by our unpreparedness, that allow us to hear the voice of God and follow His lead (which may look like a spontaneous song, a verse from the Bible, a corporate prayer, or even a simple word of encouragement to help focus the congregation)."

"You can't jump start something like this. Worship needs to be part of the musician's life style. Singing the psalms at home, playing worship songs, and then allowing yourself to sing songs over your own life, family, or your church family members are examples of the worship lifestyle. As the musician lives life in this way, they can then stand with confidence, because their cup is full and the overflow runs out of their life.

A prophetic worship leader and team also need to develop a heart for the people they serve, they need to be involved in the life of the church, so that they can understand they are called firstly to worship the King of Kings, and that their call is to allow God to use them to touch lives through their playing and singing."

There is a great need for worship pastors to mentor the next generation. We all need to be secure enough to want those we train to surpass us in creative, spiritual and natural ability. It is not our position or gift to hold onto. If we take the attitude that it's *ours* to hold onto, it becomes old and stale. When we release and give out all that we have been given, we allow the Holy Spirit to continue to breathe fresh life into and through us. We desire that many generations to come will benefit from the training and mentoring received from those that have gone before them.

One worship leader posted online: "My heart is that we would raise up a generation of artists who, under the influence of the Holy Spirit and able to hear His voice, will respond to him through their own unique creative expression."

CHAPTER 20

TEACHING A BIBLE SCHOOL CLASS ON PROPHECY

Our Bible Training School educates students both academically, and with practical hands-on ministry. Most of the students are young adults. I was asked to develop and teach a class on the prophetic for second year students; I focus on establishing the principles for prophetic ministry, but also bring in some of the practical activities I use with our prophetic teams. The prophetic is an excellent practical tool for students when they head off to do ministry. In many of the situations encountered on mission trips, the ability to prophesy has been a strong complement to outreach, evangelism and prayer.

Example: One of the students was on a ministry team, working with the Dream Centre in Los Angeles, California. On Friday night, a team went to a main strip where the clubs are located. The group had been taught to pay attention to any nudges from the Holy Spirit where they might feel there is a certain person to talk to or specific words to say. This particular student saw a beautiful girl standing outside the club, and felt that she needed to tell her: God loves you." As soon as she spoke to the girl, more words came to her—words of comfort and about God's heart of love towards her. She spoke the words over the girl. Although 'Barbie-like' on the outside, this girl was very broken on the inside. She began to cry, then sob, as God's words were spoken over her. Her "boyfriend" came along, and she refused to go with him, saying, "No, I love what this girl is saying to me!"

Receiving training in prophecy and listening for God's voice gave that student the courage to approach the 'Barbie' girl. Many times God only gives us the opening sentence or phrase, but once we are obedient to what we've been shown, He gives us more to the message.

Because I work full time, I had to schedule the class early in the morning so I could still get to work; some years we started as early as 7:00 am. The first few times I taught the class I knew the enemy was hopping mad, as I had weird things go wrong all the time. Our water line broke flooding our basement. I had car accidents and we would get unexpected bills coming seemingly out of nowhere. Don't be surprised if these types of things happen to you, particularly when you work towards equipping others with serious tools for use in God's Kingdom. I was paid a small honorarium for teaching the class, but it never offset the expense for damages by the end of the term.

Teaching the classes also gave me an opportunity to identify students with strong prophetic gifting, enabling me to later ask those students to help me in other ministry situations. Two students that I taught became part of our regular Sunday between-service prophetic ministry. I really like having young people involved, and try to include students in other prophetic opportunities that come up during the term. Older people are in awe that God is using young people with such depth for their age. Other young adults are inspired seeing students operating in a prophetic ministry capacity. I have had students take the class, go back to their home churches, and start leading prophetic teams. In fact, some requests for prophetic ministry workshops have come from former students who are now in ministry at other churches.

We should never underestimate what our sacrifice of time and energy to teach and mentor others will accomplish. An important goal is to always help others become all that they can be for Christ. I have also learned that it's not the students who are the most prophetically gifted that are actually applying what they learned, but those who really catch a vision for what teams are able to do in a local church setting. My desire is that some of those students would take the prophetic further, wider and deeper than I ever will.

CHAPTER 21

WORKSHOPS

Various churches will invite or request us to come and give a day's workshop with the "prophetic people." Often these workshops follow an earlier preaching ministry from our pastor in which he recommends either prophetic teaching or prophetic ministry. It is a great situation when church leaders have confidence in their people to recommend them and send them out. This is a privilege that I do not take for granted, as I meet many prophetic people who are frustrated in their relationships with church leadership. I'm convinced that most difficulties in these relationships come from misunderstanding, and could be resolved if churches had a prophetic team providing a platform for communication, as well as for growth and development.

We have used the following workshop format for years—it seems to work well:

One day workshops

- Bring along someone wanting to learn or to be mentored in the prophetic.

- Ask other strong team members to do some of the teaching.

- Begin with an overview of what prophecy is, and what God intends us to do with the gift of prophecy.

- Emphasize the scripture that says "*you may all prophesy*" (1 Corinthians 14: 31 NAS). Most of the people who come to a workshop are not sure if they really have a gift of prophecy or not. I always tell them to attend and see how it goes. I use interest as an indicator as usually the person is being led more prophetically than they realize. They often don't recognize their gift because it feels natural to them.

- Teach on "How God Speaks." This goes into visions, dreams, seeing words, impressions, songs and other ways God uses to speak to us. We also teach that God desires a relationship with us in which he continually speaks to us, but many times we don't recognize his voice. I use the illustration of Samuel as a child. When God called him, he kept running to Eli to ask what he'd said. Finally, after several times, Eli told Samuel that it was God speaking. I think God's voice was such an ordinary and familiar voice to Samuel that he just had to find out how to recognize it. I believe that's how it is for many prophetic people. When I first began to prophesy, I didn't have a model to follow. I was baptized with the Holy Spirit in 1978, and started getting words coming to me so strongly I felt I had to burst them out in whatever setting I was in. Then I also started to get a lot of pictures, especially when praying for someone. This wasn't particularly comfortable for me, as I didn't have a frame of reference for the pictures, and began to worry that I might be crazy. I don't regret these difficult seasons of misunderstanding, as it is part of what motivates me to want to help people develop their own prophetic gifting. In our workshops, we spend an hour or so teaching and then move into the most important part, the practical activity.

- Practical Activity: I have adapted an activity from Graham Cooke's teaching, and can't count how many times I have used it over the years. It's still the best activity that I know of for helping people overcome lack of confidence in hearing from God for someone else. We begin by writing a prayer to the person they are partnered with—something encouraging. I try to partner people who don't know each other, so as to avoid any chance that familiarity might produce the result. You want them to be specific about what they are writing, adding in a scripture, a picture or whatever they have.

Once people have written out their prayer, you can direct them to go back and reword it, shaping it the way God would write it in the first person. Essentially, they are writing out a prophecy. Then they share the word with their partner and receive feedback about it. Countless times, I have seen people walk out of this activity so encouraged, not because they received an encouraging prophecy, but because it was confirmed that the words *they* gave were just what the other person needed to hear. They thought they might have heard God in the past, but now they know for sure! They have direct confirmation from the person they were partnered with. I find that in the area of the prophetic, many people have had some teaching, but really lack in application. Working on the practical is very necessary. You need to give feedback, which can be awkward, but people really don't grow without it. Also, many people have a false picture of their gifts; working through a practical activity can expose delusions. (This is addressed more specifically in the Prophetic Arts section.)

• Allow time for questions; this is vital. People in outlying areas just don't get the opportunity for direct contact with a prophetic teacher often, and have genuine concerns and questions. Many of the battles that prophetic people have are similar, and it really helps to know that there are common struggles, and how they can be overcome. There is so much 'self-talk' that has to be aligned and submitted to the Spirit of God to allow for growth in prophecy. These are the kind of things that can be discussed within a workshop.

- Teach on the relationship between prophetic people and the leadership of the local church. I don't believe prophetic people will succeed if they try to push their way on the leaders. Prophetic people need to work at establishing a trust, while leaders have to allow prophetic people to grow and develop. Prophetic people can be impatient, wanting things to happen 'yesterday,' but they must first build a good relationship with the church leadership. If they fail to do so, things won't move ahead, and the prophets will often become cynical and critical. They lose the opportunity to develop a pure prophetic gift, and the church loses a person who could have been a real blessing.

Hosting a Workshop

Some churches find it cheaper to pay for a group of their prophetic people to travel to our church, rather than bring a team out. We only charged a $10.00 registration fee to cover the donuts and coffee. We did ask people sign up ahead of time for planning purposes.

Hosting a Prophetic Conference

Some of the workshop topics we've used:
- Prophetic worship
- Prophetic dance
- Prophetic intercession
- Personal prophecy
- Hearing God's voice
- Prophetic art expression
- Prophetic drumming & percussion
- Prophetic evangelism

Prophetic writing / poetry

Many people come to workshops from local and outlying churches. The informal building of relationships was just as important as the sessions. After the workshops, some people came in regularly to attend our prophetic team meetings. They were from a town three hours away, taking a great deal of effort and commitment. This just demonstrates how eager people are for prophetic training that is balanced and relevant. All of the sessions went really well except for prophetic art. We attempted to stir people's creative prophetic expression, but perhaps it's too much for most adults to engage in that level of interaction and participation with people they do not know.

Benefits of workshops:

> Provides a learning experience for those teaching the workshops. You may be gifted in one area, but it's entirely another thing to teach and pass along your understanding.

> Gives recognition and a bit more weight to the prophetic, as people respect that there is active practical training. Even if they aren't involved, the congregation feels more secure when they recognize that things aren't just improvised or superficial.

> Connecting with others who operate in the same gifting is refreshing for many. Some come with ideas about different prophetic expressions, but have never seen them in operation.

CHAPTER 22

CONSIDERATIONS FOR PROPHETIC MINISTRY TO OTHER CHURCHES

When ministering prophetically in other churches, it is vital to establish guidelines upfront and ensure you manage their expectations. Churches unfamiliar with prophetic ministry or those having preconceived ideas about prophetic ministry often come with unrealistic expectations. This not only hinders effective ministry, but often contributes to skepticism about prophecy. Because of this, as well as for clarity and order, it is important to establish guidelines before accepting an invitation to minister.

Typically, we'll receive a request from the pastor of a church. The pastor's focus is primarily on the needs of his or her congregation, and as a result, they often overlook or are unaware of the practical requirements for effective prophetic ministry.

I use the following as our guidelines:

1. ***Ensure the church is prepared for ministry:*** Provide the pastor a list of things to do in the weeks before the scheduled ministry. This is the same material as we distribute prior to ministering in our own Home Groups. I also suggest that the pastor teach or arrange for teaching on prophecy prior to our session. This makes the ministry more effective, as the people are prepared, and come in with the expectation of hearing from God.

2. ***Agree to a schedule:*** How many sessions will there be? How many people per session? Add that up and assess whether the people you've selected on your ministry team are up to the demand. Depending how seasoned your team is, you may have to schedule more breaks.

3. ***Ministry time:*** Blocks of about two and a half hours per session seem to work well. Even with a couple of songs, you can minister to about six sets of people. A set is a couple or a single person. You could have four couples and two to three singles or any combination that allows about twenty minutes for each set. What often happens is that you will do your agreed on 'set', and the pastor will ask you to just take one more single, or one more couple. It might be fine for me to stretch myself to do that, but I'm often ministering with someone younger, and not as experienced. It can be too much demand without a break, and I find that many times pastors are unaware of proper etiquette in these things, or do not recognize the limitations or demands upon those prophesying.

4. ***Schedule Breaks:*** Allowing for appropriate breaks is very important. Agree to a location for breaks between sessions away from the congregation. Ask that refreshments be provided. The ministry team needs time to catch their breath and avoid people trying to get a word outside of the structured meetings. I've had pastors agree to the refreshment break and the number of candidates to be ministered to, but on the break "introduce" me to someone they are hoping I'll prophesy over. We want to work hard for those we are ministering to, but that must include appropriate breaks. When people get tired, they can get sloppy in their prophecy. They take more risks and are more subject to inaccuracy. I consider breaks to be a safety feature, and best discussed at the time

you begin negotiating terms, rather than trying to deal with it in the ministry situation.

5. *Make childcare available:* Make arrangements for children so they aren't running around or clinging to their parents while the ministry is going on. It's distracting for both parents and the ministry team.

6. *Arrange for sessions to be recorded:* A simple audio recording is sufficient. These recordings need to be available to those receiving prophecy as soon as possible after the sessions. For most, the ministry time is a significant and emotional experience. Some are nervous about the ministry or distracted by the process. It's impossible for them to remember all the details of their word. A recording provides the opportunity to review and reflect in another environment. The recipient can also review the prophecy months, even years later, and track their progress or identify things they may have missed that has hindered their growth.

7. *Start each session with worship:* This does not need to be long or elaborate. A worship leader with a guitar or keyboard and two or three songs are sufficient. Worship helps to move us into the presence of God and opens up our spirits so everyone is more receptive to the Holy Spirit.

8. *Have people available to pray:* Ideally, have a group dedicated to praying for the sessions long before the team arrives. I also want people available to take each individual aside and pray for them right after they have received prophecy. This allows the team to continue ministering, and makes the most effective use of their time and energy.

9. ***Ensure church leaders and elders are present during the prophetic ministry:*** Leaders are an important resource to provide advice and direction as we prophesy. The ministry time is also a significant opportunity for leaders to discover God's call upon the lives of people in their congregation. Sometimes you sense a specific call to ministry when prophesying over an individual, but you're unsure about the timing of the word. The local leadership should help you determine how imminent the call is. As a result you will be more confident, and feel liberated to give a fuller description of what you are hearing prophetically. I've heard people say that asking questions takes away from supernatural revelation, but I think it adds value. It helps focus the prophetic word and gives the leaders an opportunity to participate in the future development of those receiving prophesy.

10. ***Identify candidates for ministry:*** Ask the pastor if there are key people who want or would benefit from ministry. Encourage the pastor to include existing leaders as well as ones who show potential for leadership. Couples and singles should be mixed throughout the ministry session. This gives variety to both the team ministering and the people supporting them. It provides more cohesiveness to the ministry and helps people see that God really does put people where He sees fit. We don't want to give the impression that the church is a couple's-only club. If the pastor also wants to call others for ministry who have not been identified as part of the schedule, make sure that it is factored into the time block. Sometimes you may be given a whole session (six - eight people per grouping) and after that, be asked to call people out for prophecy, which can significantly add to the ministry time.

11. *Travel expenses & honorariums:* We do not charge a fee for prophetic ministry, but we believe it is appropriate and biblical for our expenses to be covered. Hotel rooms are not necessary if there are adequate billeting facilities. If the ministry stretches over several days or the schedule is really packed in a single day, a hotel is preferable. This way, the team can get a bit of down time between sessions. Often when you are billeted, you spend your time talking to the hosts and getting involved in their personal problems or issues with the church. Once I was billeted in a lovely older lady's home who was a real servant, and wanted desperately to have me in her home. Her husband was a chain smoker, so the house was filled with a cloud of blue smoke. He was also deaf and had the TV blasting as loud as the volume could go. I did settle to sleep once the TV was turned off and then at 2:00 am, I was awakened by the blast of what sounded like a train going through my room. The husband couldn't sleep and got up to watch more TV with the volume full blast, until the wife got him to go back to bed. I had a full day's workshop to present and I was rattled after the night in this house. Another time the pastor's wife and I went to do a woman's conference on a reservation in Montana. The family that hosted us were lovely, but when we were shown our rooms, we were given a bunk bed in the kids' room with kids in the other set of bunks. Some people don't realize the need for a room to yourself, with possibly fruit and water available, so you have quiet place between the ministry sessions to rest and prepare for ministry.

I don't ask for a specific honorarium when ministering alone. If I come with a team, I do appreciate a financial gift that I can pass on to the team members. Often, because of the travel involved, they are taking at least a day off work without pay to go out and minister. If a church does not have specific guidelines for honorariums, I usually refer them to our pastor or one of our elders for guidance.

12. Set some specific guidelines about how you will minister and who is eligible for prophetic ministry. I use the following criteria:

a) Don't prophesy over children.

I have had children pushed into chairs for ministry when their parents aren't even present. I have had to politely explain that I won't prophesy over the children unless their parents and the pastor or elder who is requesting the ministry are present. I want to consult with them before prophesying. I don't encourage prophetic ministry to children in public. Even though a call on a person's life does often begin in childhood, we must remember that they are still children, and prophesying that they will be a pastor or leader at a young age doesn't benefit their development. I have been in prophecy situations where the prophet will ask parents if they have children and then give a related word, which is fine. If it is older teenagers or young adults, add them to the list separately.

b) Prophesy over unmarried couples individually.

I have had situations where a pastor wants me to prophesy over "about to be engaged couples," hoping that we would confirm or cancel the engagement. I have also been asked to prophesy over couples who are dating. Prophesying over the couple gives endorsement that their relationship is of God, and I feel that other criteria should be in place to discern that. I don't want the couple to say that because they were prophesied over together, it proves God is telling them to get married. It may happen that when the couple is prophesied over as individuals, their words may line up nicely for a lifelong partnership. This is a safety feature.

c) Prophesy over married couples together.

Some couples want separate ministry and it begs the question why. Sometimes it indicates a lack of trust and unity in their marriage. Practically, it takes less time to minister to the couple together rather than separately. It's easier to prophesy when you have both of them together and you can go back and forth between the husband and wife. This way you can identify how their gifts complement one another, and it confirms that God has put the two of them together. Sometimes as you are prophesying over one partner, the Holy Spirit shows you something for the spouse. It creates a nice flow in prophecy to be able to "juggle" the words between the couple.

I go out of my way to be as accommodating as I can, and build a good working relationship with church leaders. These guidelines help establish a good dialogue and realistic expectations for the ministry time. They also allow me to manage the prophetic team I'm ministering with, and make sure they are as effective as possible. The end result is a better experience for everyone. The church is well prepared for ministry, and receives it in an organized manner. Church leaders gain real insight into their people, and become aware of opportunities for growth and development. And finally, people come away inspired and encouraged to move on with God.

ABOUT THE AUTHOR:
A PROPHETIC PROFILE

The purpose of this section is to enable those who are **prophetically gifted to relate**, and **those who are not prophetically gifted to have some better understanding** of those who are.

My husband and I got saved in the late seventies, just as the "Jesus people" movement was coming to an end. That movement didn't have a lot to do with our personal salvation, except that it was the foundation of the church we eventually belonged to. My husband and I had been married for just one year when we decided as a family that we were going to confront his mother with the fact that her drinking was out of control, and that we weren't going to pretend any longer—she had a drinking problem. As it turned out, she was more than willing to admit she had a problem and in fact, wanted a way out—she was ready for change. She went into a treatment centre along with her husband, my father in law, where they had to live for one month. My dad was the supervisor of that addictions centre. Talk about polar opposites in background. My father-in-law was a district liquor sales manager and my dad was an addictions counsellor/supervisor. When my mother-in-law took the first step in AA, and gave her life and will over to God, she prayed that prayer to Jesus, whom she knew as God from during childhood. When she took that step, a chain of miracles happened in the family. Todd's mom was instantly delivered from alcoholism and within six months, her husband, daughter, three sons and wives all came to know Jesus. It was an amazing time, and these miracles were not uncommon in the late seventies.

For the first few months after Todd and I came to faith in Christ, we went to two churches plus Al-anon meetings. We had one night free during the week, and we just thought that's how Christians lived. We attended Al-anon to be supportive of Todd's mom, but finally clued in that we needed a spiritual base for our own lives. So we attended the Anglican Church because that was where his parents attended, and they had new pastors—a husband /wife team who were charismatic Christians. At the same time, we attended another church (where we still are today), because my boss had 'Bible thumped' me every day for six months, so once we had an encounter with the Lord we recognized that we needed to belong to a Bible believing church. After a while we settled into just one local church, where we have belonged ever since.

My husband Todd and I were baptized with the Holy Spirit almost as soon as we gave our lives to the Lord. Immediately I began to speak in tongues, but I also encountered the Holy Spirit in another way: I remember praying in our living room—Todd, my mother in law and I, on the floor (we only had pillows for furniture), and the room being filled with a tremendous white light and the presence of God so thick I could hardly breathe. Today I compare it to a "Book of Acts" experience. The odd thing was that Todd and his mom couldn't see the white light the same as I could, so I kept describing it to them. After that encounter, when I would be praying or in a church service, I began to get words coming to me seemingly out of nowhere. Along with the words, I'd have a compulsion to speak them out, whether we were in the Anglican Church service or at a prayer meeting. I had neither heard nor seen prophecy, so I just thought this was part of the experience of being a Christian. Shortly after that, I began to see pictures over people when we would pray for them and it was uncomfortable, because of my lack of understanding. I wondered secretly if I was crazy. Fortunately my boss, who had become a friend and mentor, explained that I had a prophetic gift, and that it was written about in the Bible. Before long, I was able to see and hear prophecy being given by others in the charismatic church we were attending, so it didn't seem quite so weird.

The church also had some prophets come in for a church presbytery, and for three nights we sat captivated by the fact that God used these men to speak very accurately to people regarding their day to day lives. I wasn't immediately propelled into prophetic ministry, and for many years I wasn't really developing my gift. There just wasn't a lot of material available about prophecy. I did get a few books that gave me more understanding, but it took many years before I realized that this gift I had was more than the everyday level of prophecy. And while I realized that I had a gift, I didn't take it all that seriously, because it was awkward. I never seemed to know the timing of giving the word, or where it should be given. I didn't see many women involved in prophecy, and I wished God had given me a quieter gift. I always felt like a bull in a China shop. Even though we fit in as a couple, and had many new couple-friends, I just didn't seem to fit in with the church women for many years. I was educated, had a career, no children and no real desire to have children when we became Christians.

The truth was, at the time we came to faith in Christ, our one-year marriage was shaky. We were so opposite in personality and had no understanding of God's plan for marriage. You would have classified me as a pure "truth" person and my husband as pure "mercy." Somehow we muddled through those first years, with God doing much work in our lives and our marriage. Todd was quick to sign up for Bible School, and eagerly drank in the Word of God. I was way more casual. My attitude was to focus on my strengths, and let God look after the rest. I used to think my husband was a bit gloomy when he'd talk about suffering and hardship being part of the walk with Christ. I had to learn the hard way that no one gets to be used in ministry unless you get on the potter's wheel and let Him shape and reshape you. I spent a lot of years avoiding that wheel and having a superficial level of Christianity as a result. Somewhere early on we went to an evening church service, and as soon as the pastor started to preach, I started to sob. I didn't know what was going on, but I was emotionally aching as I felt drawn to the Lord and what He was requiring of us. There was an altar call for those who were called to five-fold ministry and I pulled my husband to the front. We thought it was a call to a deeper level of commitment, and when we discussed it with the pastor, he told us that sometimes the wife is more sensitive to the call of God. Later Todd and I presented ourselves to the church leadership as being willing to go to Columbia as missionaries. Our offer was refused, but we thought the altar call that night was related to missions. Todd has been an elder for many years, which may have been what that five-fold ministry call was about. In the past couple of years, as I reflect on that night, I realize that may have been my call to become a prophet—although I wouldn't have understood that at the time. My mission now is to train up people in the prophetic, just as strongly as it is my mission to prophesy.

There was a great presence of God in those services when we first came to know God. We drank it up, along with the strong teaching on local church and the purposes of the Kingdom of God. There were many prayer opportunities—almost every service—and as Todd was set in as an elder, we would often be called to come forward and pray for people. Todd would tell me to come forward and pray with him, and for a long time I would resist, saying I had nothing for this person. He would grab my hand and make me come forward. As soon as I would lay my hands on someone, I would begin to get prophetic words. It took me a while to realize that as we give ourselves in prayer and obedience, God has opportunity to show up and speak clearly to us. I didn't connect how important it was for me to be in close prox- imity with the person, or better yet, to just lay my hand lightly on their shoulder—then I could prophesy. The other thing that would happen is when we were praying in a group for someone, I could hear clearly, unless someone put their hand on me, and then I would get almost agitated. It would distract me from hearing for the first person, and I would go onto hearing for the person whose hand was on me. Lots of times, in my 'not so subtle' way, I would throw the person's hand off my back so I could continue prophesying for the individual. I'm sure a lot of people were very confused about me!

Our three children were born between 1980 and 1986. I worked outside of the home, plus was very involved with the church in home group ministry and whatever else was going on, including the prophetic ministry by then. Todd was an elder, and taught in the Christian School.

In 1986, the pastor of our church had to be removed against his will, due to moral failure. We had a "sister" church in another city of which the pastor's son was the senior pastor. It was discovered that both father and son were in moral failure at the same time. Many people from our congregation had been sent out to that sister church as part of a church plant, and many of us went back and forth to preach and lend a hand to start the second church. When the issues were exposed of moral failures on both pastors' part, there was terrible devastation in lives where there had been so much hope and promise. We couldn't believe something like this would happen in the church.

We were also in a church building project that had been mishandled, and the pastor who was removed left the church with a 1.8 million dollar debt. The good things that came out of all of that were that we humbled ourselves, realizing that we had become proud and legalistic as a church, and that we got wonderful new pastors, who remain part of the pastoral team to this day. Needless to say, it took at least two years for the church to be turned around and start becoming healthy again. We lost some friends who crashed at that time —we are still praying for their restoration. It seemed that those who stayed with the church got healed, and basically those that left, didn't. The pain of it all still brings tears to my eyes as I write. I'm thankful for the experience because it has made our Christianity so much more real, but if I had to choose to go through it again, I don't think I could.

During that time, my prophetic gift seemed to be rising to a new level. I remember one healing service shortly before our new pastors came, as people came forward in a ministry prayer line, I had a word for every single person. It was beginning to dawn on me that maybe I was called to a prophetic ministry, and not just the occasional use of the prophetic gift.

In those years I made mistakes, and can be thankful for the grace of the leadership in the church, especially the pastor and elders. One time in a service, shortly after the former pastor had been removed, I prophesied in a Sunday service that there were wolves amongst us, attacking sheep, causing them to bleed, etc. I use that now as an example of a word that should be submitted to the leadership and should not have been given publically. The result, of course, was that everyone was looking at one another, trying to figure out who was the wolf amongst us. These words brought insecurity into the sheepfold (the church), and shouldn't have been given publically. The pastor had to immediately make an adjustment to that word, to tame it down and bring it to a prayer focus. Again, this shows that I was lacking in understanding of how to handle the prophetic gift. While I think the word was accurate, I lacked prophetic etiquette.

Another time I was prophesying over a man in a home group setting, and I was very distressed over what I could see happening in his life. He was so unresponsive that I felt like he was dangling over hell, and about to lose his family and his relationship with God. As I was emphatically prophesying, I was hitting him on the back over and over, until my husband grabbed a hold of my hand to stop me. I wasn't intentionally doing this, but I was overcome with the intensity of the power of the prophetic spirit on me, and I didn't know how to handle it. I was always afraid if I didn't give the word that I wouldn't be found faithful, and I would be letting God down. It took me several years to realize that God has several ways to speak to people, and when I read the account of Balaam and the donkey, I realized that God can resort to using a donkey if He has to. So, if I miss it or get it wrong sometimes, it's not shaking God up. I am so thankful to God for the encouragement to prophesy—particularly from my husband, the elders and pastors—and I realize I wouldn't have grown and developed without it.

We had a prophet, named Keith Hazel, assigned to give prophetic oversight to our church. He was wonderful to me, as he understood my struggles to get it right, and helped me not to take myself so seriously. I have seen him in a prophetic ministry situation toss popcorn in the air and try and catch it with his mouth between sentences. Prophecy feels so natural to him that it was like breathing; he could eat and give revelatory prophecy all at the same time. He is very balanced with his gift, and watching him, I was finally able to relax a little bit. I was able to see that we don't always have to be so intense about our gift, but can actually enjoy using our gift of prophecy.

One area in the prophetic that I struggled with for about 15 fifteen years was that after I prophesied, I would analyze the prophecy to death. I would review what I thought was God, what I thought might be mixture of God and me, and where I thought I'd missed it. This was an exhausting process, as I was prophesying regularly through most of this time. I was very hard on myself, and my husband, full of mercy, would regularly have to encourage me that I hadn't gotten it wrong, that the word sounded good, that it built up the service or individual. God really had to give me a breakthrough in this area, and He finally got through to me that if I was faithful to speak what He gave me to the best of my ability, the results were up to Him.

I also began to realize that I was basing my assessment of how good or bad the prophecy was on the feedback of others. If I gave a word and no one said anything to me about it, I would assume that the word was weak, or didn't speak to people's hearts or was just 'off'. If I gave a word and got lots of feedback, I would be on cloud nine, so happy the word had been received. After a while, I realized that this was a harmful and immature way of looking at things. People just forget to give feedback sometimes. It's not a measure of the prophetic word. Measuring myself against the feedback was just causing me to be in a constant cycle of self-examination. Since God set me free of this thinking, I have been able to function in much more liberty and grow in the prophetic. I leave the results with Him.

I've learned that we can't really measure the impact of prophecy anyway. Sometimes the thing you almost don't bother to say is the thing that will mean the most to someone, whereas the burning part of the word may just be sloughed off. It doesn't matter. I totally want to be accountable for any error or misjudgement in the prophetic, but I no longer feel overly responsible for every word I give. I prophesy all the time, and I just say "God it's all yours: the good, the bad and the ugly." I believe God is big enough to handle the results, and my job is to hear the best I can and be the messenger. God is a mighty God, and prophecy is only one tool he is using to work in people's lives. I believe it is a significant tool and a good one, but He isn't limited to work in people solely through prophecy. Somehow this realization, which came so late for me, has been ever so freeing, and caused me to actually enjoy prophesying. I enjoy it and I look forward to a whole weekend of prophetic immersion where I can just give myself to prophesy. I love it, and know this is what I was created to do! Too bad I wasted years trying to make myself something I wasn't. Being so untrained myself in the early years has given me a passion to train young people in the prophetic.

Getting Stretched in the Use of the Gift

Over the years, God stretched my tolerance both as a person and in my prophetic gift. I quite often ministered at women's conferences, and also taught prophetic workshops and ministered prophetically. This usually involved travel and billeting, meaning that I would be two days totally immersed with other people, including sleeping. If you were to meet me, you would think I was an extrovert, as I am outgoing and enjoy meeting new people. That is basically what I'm like, but it's time-limited, and then I need to pull away to get my thoughts together, and not be somewhere that something is demanded of me. If I can pull away, even for a little while, I can rein myself in and get back into the flow of the weekend. My husband of course is a true extrovert, and he doesn't like to leave the church until he has greeted everyone there. When we were first married our differences were more magnified, and one time, I just couldn't take talking to one more person, so I took the car and went home leaving him to catch a ride. I will just say I never did that again. This example shows how short my tolerance was, so it was a big stretch for me to be with people twenty-four hours a day on these ministry trips. It seemed that the line-ups at the altar never ended. You'd think you were near the end and more people would pop up. I didn't realize for a long time that when people were coming to me asking for prayer, they wanted a prophetic word. I could only prophesy so long and then I started getting clouded in what I was seeing and hearing. I discovered that I needed to tell people that I would pray for them but I wouldn't prophesy, because we had been ministering for two hours already.

One time I was at a woman's conference, sharing a room, and I went to lock myself in the bathroom to escape for a few minutes. It was a brand new hotel, and every time I went to the room for a little break, a repairman was in the room; they were fixing the bathroom, replacing something in the heating ducts. I was really over the edge and finally asked them to leave while I cried in the bathroom for half an hour to get a grip. Finally over the years, I developed a better tolerance for so much 'togetherness.' If I'm asked my preference for accommodations, I will still take a hotel. What happens when you're billeted is that you are already handling a demanding ministry schedule and then you go to people's places and they want personal ministry on top of it all. Now when I'm being billeted, I ask ahead that I have my own room and a place to work and pray. That at least helps me give my best to the meetings.

Another time I was doing a prophetic workshop in a city two and a half hours away. The ministry started on Friday evening. I had worked at my job until about 3:00, and then I picked up the women who were coming with me. I was conscious of mentoring people, so I took three women along with me. I drove, and when we got to the meeting I was just changing in the bathroom at the church, and they were pounding on the door for me to come up so they could get started. I taught and prophesied over women that night for three and a half hours.

When we finished up the evening, I was so looking forward to getting to the billet house, and to finally having some space, only to find out that I had to share a bed with one of the women who came with me. That woman has a very bubbly personality and never stopped talking. I thought I was going to die, which is maybe what God had in mind (in the dying to self-interest sort of way). I taught and ministered all the next day, then we jumped in the car and I made the drive home to my family by 7:00 pm and started all the weekend chores that needed doing before Monday. I learned a lesson on that trip: I don't have to try to be superwoman. From then on, if I was booked for ministry, I at least took the afternoon off from work, if not the whole day. I don't drive; I have someone else do it, and I only take women with me who are calm. The last couple of years, I've tried to have my husband, daughter or best friend come with me as a support. I can give my best that way.

It just seemed like my tolerance for people and ministry trips was improving, then God went to work on stretching me prophetically. I think he took me from being a relay runner, and trained me to be a long distance runner, and it's not over yet. We worked in teams whenever we were asked to do prophetic ministry in the church, and outside. I always did the planning and scheduling for those times, and still do the majority of it. I had to learn to oversee the teams ministering, and minister myself at the same time, so it's sort of like keeping your own heart rate going while you are checking everybody else's pulse in the room. If everyone stuck to the plans made ahead of time for the ministry, things would go fairly smoothly. Often people get attacked with sickness or a family situation before the ministry event, so now I usually have a couple of people 'on deck,' just in case. I am also more assertive when I see the teams getting stretched too much; I will say we need a break, or we can only do one more set that night. Just because God has stretched me to handle a fairly good ministry load doesn't mean those that are being trained up can handle the same thing. It's like Moses in the wilderness, when his father-in-law had to tell him to pace himself for the weaker members in order to survive the trip.

I had a recent reminder that people have to build up stamina in order to minister for a whole evening session: the Sunday 'between-services' ministry we are doing with the Intermediate Teams requires them to minister to three to four people successively, which is a stretch for Intermediate level people. It reminded me that it takes years to build up the ability to minister for long periods at one time. Two years ago I was invited on a ministry trip to Taiwan. It was ten days of ministry without breaks, and included a combination of prophesying, teaching and preaching. We ministered individually to groups of twelve to fifteen in a block of time. It wasn't supposed to be that many but they kept adding into the schedules. We also had to minister by ourselves. I was assigned a room with an interpreter and ten to twelve people waiting for me. It was me and them, basically staring at me with expectation in their faces. I had the lead prophet's wife come with me for moral support, as I had rarely ministered by myself since we believed in and worked in teams. It was a gruelling schedule; we did at least two groups of prophetic ministry per day, and then we might need to teach or hold a service at night. God's grace was definitely there, but it was like an endurance test. I was so grateful for every time in the past where I'd had to minister when it was inconvenient, when things went later than they should have, and for every single bit of ministry I had ever done to prepare me for this marathon. Several things happened to me on that trip:

1. I proved to myself that through God's grace, I could do this— that I was up for the task. (The enemy had been nagging at me, telling me that I wasn't up to this scale of ministry.)

2. My faith level was increased, and I understood that God's well doesn't run dry. That was a secret fear I'd had—that I'd be expected to prophesy, and wouldn't have anything to say for someone.

3. I felt like I had put a stake in the ground for women in ministry. There were several women at that conference needing to see a woman taking her place, in a respectful way. I hadn't pushed to be there, God opened the door. In many situations, women don't get to have or be role models. Even in this day and age, I am a curiosity to some people.

4. I was pushed forward to preach in healing/prophetic services. We then took turns calling people out and prophesying over them. In a country where Taoism and Buddhism were promi- nent, God got their attention through words of knowledge and miracles. We saw some powerful things happen in those ser- vices, and I was more determined than ever to bring the super-

natural realm into all our ministries at home.

5. I found out that I loved it all—the challenge and the variety. It was a perfect combination of prophesying, teaching, encouraging, building people up and preaching prophetically. I'd do it again in a heartbeat, even with all the demands, inconvenience and stretching required.

Since that ministry experience, I am not shying away from opportunities as I might have in the past. I am pushing myself into deeper waters. I've had it prophesied over me many times that the Lord is willing to take me as deep as I want to go, that He is not going to put limits on my ministry but it will be me who decides how deep. I am more willing to believe that since the Taiwan experience. In the past two years there have been some situations and challenges that I wouldn't have been able to handle if I hadn't been there.

Last year I was invited in to be a part of a presbytery at a church outside our stream of churches. I felt it was a 'God opportunity' and I accepted, taking my daughter with me. When I got there, I found out I was the lead in the ministry team, and had to direct the weekend of ministry and take the lead prophesying. I didn't back down from it, and I knew what to do. If that had happened before my Taiwan trip, I would have really had to battle intimidation, which would have limited my effectiveness that weekend.

Another ministry trip this year required me to prophesy alone. There was another prophet there, but because the ministry schedule was so intense, he decided we had to do "one offs." He would minister to one, and then I would to another. This way of ministering has always intimidated me in the past, but I found that I really liked it. It was a break when you were only expected to prophesy to every second person, so we could go longer. Sometimes the things you fear end up being your victories in God.

There are times I have wondered why God picked me to be a prophetic person, because I have a side to me that is very practical and some would say, pragmatic. I had a tremendous encounter with the Holy Spirit more than thirty years ago, and because of that encounter I value the Holy Spirit and God's presence so much. I love to be in the presence of God, and when our church had the season of the renewal movement in the nineties, I drank up that time of refreshing. Because I now so value the Holy Spirit, I have a zeal that things be done decently and in order representing the Holy Spirit. I don't enjoy conversations with people where, because I'm prophetic, they tell me the weirdest stuff and think I'm going to embrace it. I don't even understand what they are saying most of the time. I try to ask them, "How are you applying this in your life? What do you think God wants you to do with this information? Have you asked God for an interpretation?" Needless to say, I'm not altogether popular with some people. I love the prophetic and I love the supernatural, yet I feel strongly about representing the Holy Spirit well and in a practical way.

One of the girls I am mentoring in the prophetic gave me this prophetic picture, which summarizes where I am my prophetic journey:

"I saw you walking along a path in a field with a large bag of seed under your left arm, and with your right hand you were grabbing handfuls of seed and tossing it out on the ground as you were walking. You had walked a very long way and tossed a lot of seed, yet that same bag was always full and never ran empty. Your focus was to continue walking and tossing. Then I noticed there was a hole in the back of the bag and seed was leaking out behind you as you walked, but you didn't notice the hole. Then I saw the seeds on the path behind you, like watching popcorn kernels jump while they are hot. The seeds that jumped split into two seeds, making two whole seeds. Because you were forging ahead, you didn't notice that the seeds behind were multiplying. Just as Jesus multiplied the loaves and fishes, the Holy Spirit was multiplying the seeds both in your bag and on the ground. I then saw you and God on the top of either a very large hill top or mountain top, and you were standing like father and daughter, or like two best friends with one arm around one another, side by side. You and He were looking at the view from where you stood to see the fruits of your labour, and He showed you the crop that you and He had planted together, and it was amazing.

That prophecy was given to me two years ago, and I feel that this book is part of the seeds multiplying.

END NOTES

[1] Graham Cooke, *Developing Your Prophetic Gifting* (Kent: Sovereign World Ltd., 1994) pp. 199-201

[2] Larry Randolph, *User Friendly Prophecy* pp. 29-31

[3] Bill Hamon *Prophetic 101 and Prophetic 202* (www.godspeak.org)

[4] Steve Thompson, *You May All Prophesy!* (Charlotte, N.C. Morningstar Publications + Ministries, 2000)

[5] Brad Jersak, *Can You Hear Me?* (Altona Manitoba, Friesens, 2003)

[6] Graham Cooke, *Foundations of Prophecy and Developing a Supernatural Lifestyle*

[7] Kris Vallotton, *A Call To War* (Redding, CA., Bethel Church, 2004)

[8] Dr. Bill Hamon, *Prophetic Pitfalls and Principles*, (Shippensburg, PA, Destiny Image, 1991)

[9] Jim Wies *The Making of a Prophet* (www.godspeak.org)

[10] Andy Stanley, *Visioneering* (Colorado Springs, Multnomah Publishers, 1999) pp. 45-47

[11] Doug Addison, *Prophecy, Dreams, and Evangelism* (New Hampshire, Streams Publishing House, 2005) pp.78

[12] ibethel.org, *Treasure Hunts,* Online posting May 23, 2013

[13] Matt Tommey, www.theworshipstudio. blogspot.ca, April 26, 2009. Online posting May 25, 2013

[14] Dr. Bill Hamon, pp.199

[15] www.theworshipstudio.blogspot.ca Online posting June 3, 2013

Made in the USA
Coppell, TX
28 June 2020